Preparing Future Faculty in the Sciences and Mathematics

A Guide for Change

Anne S. Pruitt-Logan
Jerry G. Gaff
Joyce E. Jentoft
and Participants in the Program

Council of Graduate Schools
Association of American Colleges and Universities

Washington, DC 2002

This material is based upon work supported by the National Science Foundation under Grant No. DUE- 9813876.

Any opinions, findings, and conclusions or recommendations expressed in this material are those of the author(s) and do not necessarily reflect the views of the National Science Foundation.

Publisher: Association of American Colleges and Universities

Table of Contents

Preface

At a time when academic careers seem to be ever more demanding and uncertain, this publication offers a new vision for the preparation of college and university faculty in the sciences and mathematics. This new vision, Preparing Future Faculty (PFF), identifies teaching, research, and service as the three expectations for faculty at most institutions of higher learning and asserts that graduate students planning to join the faculty should begin learning about each of these elements of the academic profession.

This vision is a response to recent reports calling for significant change in doctoral education. *Reshaping the Education of Scientists and Engineers*, a 1995 report issued collectively by the National Academy of Science, the National Academy of Engineering, and the National Institute of Medicine, called for a "new Ph.D. degree." The degree they envisioned would cultivate a broader range of academic and career skills, offer more program options, provide students with more knowledge about a variety of careers, and foster a greater sense of entrepreneurship than is customary. That recommendation was echoed in another report by the Association of American Universities, comprised of leading research universities (Committee on Graduate Education 1998). It declares: "Student interests should be paramount in designing a graduate curriculum that prepares students for a broad array of careers," implying that current programs are sometimes too narrow and that student interests often are not paramount. The report went on to discuss a set of best practices, citing the PFF initiative as "one of the most systematic efforts to increase graduate student preparation for teaching."

Several research studies on graduate students have recently been completed, and they add a sense of urgency to the calls for change. For instance, Golde and Dore (2001, 5) drew the following conclusion.

> ...in today's doctoral programs there is a three-way mismatch between student goals, training, and actual careers. ... Doctoral students persist in pursuing careers as faculty members, and graduate programs persist in preparing them for careers at research universities, despite the well-publicized paucity of academic jobs and efforts to diversify the options available to doctorate-holders. The result: Students are not well prepared to assume the faculty positions that are available, nor do they have a clear concept of their suitability for work outside of research.

The classic problem with reports like these from both blue-ribbon commissions and research studies is the huge gulf between their recommendations and the actions of leaders of campus programs. The history of such reports is that they seldom lead to significant change.

Unlike those reports, this volume focuses on operational programs that have been designed and implemented by faculty and administrative leaders of doctoral programs and that have enrolled hundreds of graduate students who have gained valuable experience within the programs. It contains both conceptual and practical information about how to carry out some of the growing number of recommendations for the improvement of doctoral preparation for the professoriate. It also addresses the struggles to forge new programs in departments burdened with tradition and identifies the actual benefits to students, faculty members, departments, and institutions of persevering with this task.

The basis for this report is a project titled "Shaping the Preparation of Future Science and Mathematics Faculty," a four-year effort supported by the National Science Foundation. It is one of four coordinated initiatives in the PFF program co-sponsored by the Council of Graduate Schools and the Association of American Colleges and Universities. This project included work in five academic disciplines: biological and life sciences, chemistry, computer science, mathematics, and physics. In four of these areas the work was led by professional societies. The societies held national competitions to award grants to departments for developing model PFF programs in their fields. The societies highlighted these new approaches in their publications and meetings, encouraging their adoption by other institutions. This report contains the lessons learned by faculty members, graduate students, and academic administrators in establishing these innovative programs.

This volume is organized into five sections: the vision and its rationale, analyses of strategies for introducing PFF programs, illustrative content of the programs, information about the results and outcomes, and challenges for the future. These discussions point to actions that faculty members and administrators can take to improve faculty preparation. We hope that information about this new approach to doctoral preparation will encourage additional science and mathematics departments to pursue their own innovations.

The primary audience for this publication includes faculty members, academic administrators, graduate students, and others interested in the quality and preparation of college and university faculty. Others who might be interested include boards of trustees, state and national policy makers, leaders of educational associations, those who provide graduate fellowships, and anyone interested in improving the quality of graduate and undergraduate education.

Acknowledgments

We want to express our gratitude to many individuals who contributed to this project and to the preparation of this volume. Foremost are the PFF leaders who managed the work within the disciplinary societies that partnered with PFF:

- ▲ Robert Beck, professor and chair, department of computing sciences, Villanova University; chair, PFF leadership team, Special Interest Group on Computer Science Education of the Association for Computing Machinery;

- ▲ Jerry Bell, senior scientist, and Marta Gmurczyk, senior staff associate, American Chemical Society;

- ▲ Warren Hein, associate executive officer, American Association of Physics Teachers;

- ▲ Samuel M. Rankin, III, associate executive director, American Mathematical Society, Washington Office; and

- ▲ Thomas Rishel, associate executive director, Mathematical Association of America.

Faculty members who provided leadership for the PFF programs in nineteen departments of universities selected to participate in this program are listed in Appendix II. These faculty leaders helped their colleagues design new PFF programs, recruit faculty members and students in their disciplines, and implement the programs; they also shared ideas and information about their efforts to establish PFF programs that constitute the heart of this volume.

Faculty members and academic administrators at partner campuses with primary missions of undergraduate education were crucial to the operation of these PFF programs. The partner institutions provided PFF graduate students with insights about faculty and student life on their campuses. They also are listed in Appendix II. Graduate students who decided to take a chance by enrolling in an innovative program, sometimes against the advice of their research advisors, were courageous and willing to share their experiences and judgments about the value of their PFF programs.

Several colleagues at the Council of Graduate Schools (CGS) and the Association of American Colleges and Universities (AAC&U) deserve special mention. At CGS, Debra Stewart, president; Leslie Sims, dean in residence and director of external grants programs; and Tracie Fellers, PFF program manager, offered valuable assistance throughout this project. Valuable assistance at AAC&U was provided by Carol Geary Schneider, president; Alma Clayton-Pedersen, vice president for education and institutional renewal; and Charles Bashara, associate director of PFF. Veronica Thomas, professor of human development and psychoeducational studies at Howard University, was the external evaluator. Two consultants advised us as we coordinated the life sciences initiative: Karen Oates, professor of integrated studies at George Mason University, and Kathleen Parson, professor of biology and chemistry at Macalester College. Richard Weibl served as PFF program manager at AAC&U for the first two and one-half years of the project and was instrumental in its success.

For its generous support of this project, we are grateful to the National Science Foundation. We especially appreciate the support of the NSF staff, including Norman Fortenberry, director, division of undergraduate education, Directorate for Education and Human Resources, and Myles Boylan, our program officer; they were extremely helpful as we proceeded with this large, complex, and previously untried initiative.

This project was built on two earlier university-wide PFF programs funded by The Pew Charitable Trusts, with excellent leadership from Ellen Wert, program officer. During most of the life of this project, we benefited from the leadership and consultation with participants in those two previous initiatives. A subsequent project focused on developing PFF programs in the social sciences and humanities is being funded by The Atlantic Philanthropies, with strong leadership from Theodore Hullar. This latter initiative also enriched the current project.

Preparation of the Report

This report is the result of a large collaborative writing effort. Campus leaders at the doctoral-granting institutions involved in the project (familiarly known as "cluster leaders") provided responses to a number of questions posed by the national staff about their PFF programs. Executives of the disciplinary societies prepared syntheses of these reports for their individual disciplines. In October 2001, thirty-four individuals gathered in Washington, D.C. to discuss these disciplinary and cluster reports and the substance of this publication, and to add more details. Disciplinary discussion groups led by society executives included faculty leaders from nearly all nineteen graduate programs, several graduate student participants, a PFF alumnus in a faculty position, and the national PFF staff. Subsequent disciplinary draft reports were submitted to the national staff, which served as the primary writing/editorial group. We prepared an integrated draft and sent it to the executives for review and critique. When we arrived at a final draft, Bridget Puzon, editor at AAC&U, edited the manuscript, and Julie Warren, AAC&U production coordinator, transformed it into this printed volume.

To all who contributed, we are grateful.

Anne S. Pruitt-Logan, Scholar in Residence at CGS and Principal
Investigator in the Sciences and Mathematics
Jerry G. Gaff, Senior Scholar at AAC&U and Co-Principal Investigator
Joyce E. Jentoft, Scholar in Residence at CGS and Co-Principal Investigator

Washington, DC, February, 2002

Chapter 1

A New Vision of Graduate Preparation for Science and Mathematics Faculty

New faculty members in most institutions of higher learning are expected to be effective teachers, active researchers, and good academic citizens who contribute to the betterment of their departments and campuses. They are expected to be able to teach and advise a student body diverse not only in race, ethnicity, gender, and other demographic qualities, but also in terms of intellectual skills, motivation, and learning styles. Faculty and administrative colleagues expect new faculty to be able to employ powerful new strategies of teaching and learning, including collaborative, experiential, and technological approaches, and to assist with campus initiatives, such as writing across the curriculum, assessment of student learning, and strong general education curricula. These challenges face all new faculty, but they are more critical in the sciences and mathematics, where many undergraduate students lack adequate background, fear their own inadequacies, and seek to avoid these subjects altogether. Indeed, one of the greatest challenges facing colleges and universities today is preparing all students to live and function in a new era, a world where technology and unprecedented scientific advances, representing both promise and peril, have proven their capacity to both connect us and shock us.

Further, a substantial reform movement exists in the sciences and mathematics to help students learn about the natural and living worlds. It involves such diverse initiatives as using problem-based learning to teach calculus, analyzing important community issues such as AIDS and pollution by means of biochemical concepts, finding engaging ways to teach non-scientists in all disciplines, assessing scientific learning and quantitative reasoning, and making scientific fields attractive to underrepresented groups. (Seymour 2002; Wubbels and Girgus 1996.)

Where in their graduate programs do aspiring faculty learn about these matters and acquire capacities to make these improvements? The answer is that too often they do not, at least not in any systematic manner. It is true that some doctoral students may become teaching assistants, and some may even discover significant talent as teachers. But the reality is that large numbers of graduate students do not have an opportunity to be teaching assistants, and many teaching assistants are not given much training or support. Many teaching assistants are relegated to low-level assignments, such as supervising laboratories, grading papers, or leading discussion sections, and don't have opportunities to grapple with the serious intellectual and practical challenges of teaching, learning, and service within an institution of higher education. The academy faces the challenge of raising the quality of faculty preparation, because teaching and professional service are frequently not components of doctoral education.

Many faculty members and administrators in doctoral education assert that American graduate education in science is the envy of the world, and they believe that all is well with their programs. And yet, after a thorough review of undergraduate education, the advisory committee to the National Science Foundation's Directorate for Education and Human Resources (1996, iii) pointed to a serious deficiency:

Despite the observation that America's basic research in science, mathematics, engineering, and technology is world-class, its education is still not. America has produced a significant share of the world's great scientists while most of its population is virtually illiterate in science. Undergraduate SME&T [science mathematics, engineering, and technology] education is typically still too much of a filter that produces a few highly-qualified graduates while leaving most of its students 'homeless in the universe.'

If undergraduate science is to be improved, doctoral students preparing for academic careers will have to learn to address this problem. New faculty will have to learn to be effective teachers, invent curricula, devise instructional strategies, and construct programs that engage students in learning.

The Preparing Future Faculty program, known familiarly as PFF, sets forth a vision of graduate preparation for new science and mathematics faculty that equips them to be leaders of twenty-first century science education. In 1998, academic departments in the biological and life sciences, chemistry, computer science, mathematics, and physics embraced the vision, and—led by their disciplinary societies—embarked on a collaboration to infuse PFF concepts into the preparation of the future professoriate.

What is PFF?

PFF is a configuration of ideas designed to promote expanded professional development of doctoral students who aspire to an academic career. It embraces the doctoral degree's traditional emphasis on research, but it also brings knowledge about the diverse colleges and universities that constitute the higher education landscape—particularly those primarily serving undergraduate students—into doctoral preparation. For those interested in a faculty career, PFF introduces students to the academic profession and to the diversity of institutions with their different missions, student bodies, and expectations for faculty. PFF gives graduate students an opportunity to experience faculty life in a protected educational context at a variety of colleges and universities, allowing them to decide if they really do want an academic career, and if so, to determine what kind of institution is right for them.

Future faculty should be given progressively more complex assignments, more responsibility, and recognition associated with increased professional capacities.

The most fundamental idea characterizing PFF is that the doctoral experience for those interested in an academic career should include: a) increasingly independent and varied teaching responsibilities, b) opportunities to grow and develop as a researcher, and c) opportunities to serve the department, campus, and community. More specific concepts include the following:

1. Apprenticeship teaching, research, and service experiences should be planned so that they are appropriate to the student's stage of professional development and progress toward the degree. Doctoral students assigned as teaching assistants, for example, tend to be viewed as "covering a course section" rather than developing professional expertise benefiting themselves and students. Future faculty should be given progressively more complex assignments, more responsibility, and recognition associated with increased professional capacities.

2. Doctoral students should learn about the academic profession through

exposure to the range of professional responsibilities in the variety of institutions that may become their professional homes. Becoming aware of the variety of institutions enables them to find a better "fit," providing them with context as they seek to match their own interests and competencies with the needs of departments and institutions.

3. Doctoral programs should include a formalized system for mentoring in all aspects of professional development. Just as students have a mentor to guide their research, they also would benefit from an ongoing relationship with an experienced faculty member as they develop their teaching and service repertoire. Indeed, students can benefit from multiple mentors. A teaching mentor may be at a different institution, perhaps one with a mission that is distinctly different from that of the research university.

4. Doctoral experiences should equip future faculty for the significant changes taking place in the classrooms and curricula of today. For example, future faculty should be competent in using technology and in addressing issues presented by increasing heterogeneity among students, sophisticated about general education and interdisciplinary curricula, and capable of using the newer, active, collaborative, technological, and experiential approaches to teaching and learning.

5. Professional development experiences should be thoughtfully integrated into the academic program and sequence of degree requirements. Unless leaders of doctoral education are intentional about these matters and structure these new experiences into their programs, PFF activities are likely to be added on to an already full program and may increase time to degree. Careful integration overcomes the tendency to add new elements without modifying existing expectations which could avoid lengthening time to degree.

6. Where high-quality teaching assistant orientation and development programs are available, PFF programs should build upon them. PFF is consistent with the best practices of teaching assistant development, while also advancing another, more comprehensive level of preparation. While teaching assistant development programs can be valuable preparation for certain faculty roles, PFF programs broaden preparation by including teaching experiences at different institutions, providing mentors for coaching and feedback, and engaging students in professional service and governance responsibilities of various sorts.

The other key element in the implementation of the PFF program is the "cluster," a new form of institutional collaboration that brings the "consumers" of Ph.D.s together with the "producers." A cluster is a formal, cooperative arrangement involving doctoral-granting universities—anchors— with a range of other institutions or departments—"partners" in our terms— in a joint working relationship. Specifically, the cluster leadership:

▲ decides what is needed in new faculty (and it is always more than specialized knowledge in a discipline);

▲ gives students opportunities to experience faculty life in multiple institutional settings; and

▲ increases awareness among faculty in both the doctoral university and partner institutions about the expectations for faculty and the ways faculty roles are changing in various institutions.

The idea is to develop PFF programs that produce students who are well prepared to meet the needs of institutions that hire new faculty.

Making the Case for the PFF Concept

In recent years a good deal of empirical study has documented the need for this new concept. Studies of graduate students (Golde and Dore 2001; Lovitts 2001; National Association of Graduate and Professional Students 2001; Nyquist, et al. 2001) support the need for more information about potential careers, greater attention to teaching, more mentoring, and a closer relationship between doctoral preparation and the realities of faculty work. Similarly, studies of new faculty point to the need for better graduate preparation and clearer expectations about the nature of faculty work (Rice, Sorcinelli, and Austin 2000; Trower 2001; Sorcinelli 2001). Studies of doctoral recipients several years after receiving their degrees, including those employed both in the academy and outside it, also support the need for new approaches represented by PFF ideas (Nerad and Cerney 1999; Nerad and Cerney 2000; Smith and Pedersen-Gallegos 2001). A summary of these studies can be found on the PFF Web site at www.preparing-faculty.org.

Why PFF and Disciplinary Associations?

In developing the third phase of the PFF program, the national PFF leadership in 1998 initiated partnerships with selected disciplinary societies in several academic disciplines as a way to gain the support of more graduate faculty and their departments. In the first phase of PFF, graduate deans received grants to organize university-wide programs. They created clusters of diverse institutions to develop model programs based on PFF concepts (see Table 1). A subsequent grant, the second phase, allowed deans to further institutionalize PFF programs, assess results, disseminate findings, and spread the PFF vision to other institutions. This strategy was successful in building a broad base of support for PFF ideas among graduate deans and within a limited

Table 1. PFF Project History

PROJECT PHASE	DATES	GOAL	FUNDING	PARTICIPANTS
I	1993-1997	Develop model programs	The Pew Charitable Trusts	17 anchor institutions and 68 institutional partners
II	1997-2002	Institutionalize and spread programs	The Pew Charitable Trusts	15 anchor institutions and 119 institutional partners
III	1998-2002	Develop model programs in the sciences and mathematics	National Science Foundation	19 departments and 92 departmental partners
IV	1999-2002	Develop model programs in the humanities and social sciences	The Atlantic Philanthropies	25 departments and 130 departmental partners

number of disciplines, notably the humanities and social sciences. Thus graduate deans led the early initiatives.

Despite this support, the total number of graduate faculty involved was limited, and academic departments did not develop a significant sense of ownership for the PFF program. Too few faculty members were aware of the changing expectations for new faculty, the current job market, and the potential benefits of PFF programs for their graduate students.

Thus, in the third phase, PFF joined with the following disciplinary societies to develop model PFF programs in academic departments of their disciplines:

▲ American Association of Physics Teachers;
▲ American Chemical Society;

▲ American Mathematical Society jointly with the Mathematical Association of America; and

▲ Special Interest Group on Computer Science Education of the Association for Computing Machinery.

Originally, a society in the biological and life sciences was included, but it withdrew because it reported little interest in PFF among its members. The national PFF office subsequently served as a surrogate for the biology association in soliciting proposals and found significant interest within universities. Appendix I provides information about graduate student enrollment, doctoral degrees awarded, and posdoctorate positions that places this PFF project within the larger context of graduate education in each discipline.

The initiative to collaborate with disciplinary societies was based on the assumption that by focusing on challenges and opportunities facing the disciplines, the societies could entice graduate faculty and their departments to look carefully at the diverse world of higher education in which new assistant professors work, and to enrich their doctoral programs accordingly. Doctoral education is a powerful socialization experience in which academic departments play primary roles. It is through doctoral education that scholars in a field of specialization educate future practitioners and cultivate their capacities to make advances in the field. These disciplinary societies have embraced PFF as an important direction for the future of doctoral education in their fields. In so doing, society leaders discovered that PFF creates synergy with other national agendas pursued by the societies, such as efforts to diversify the faculty, provide seminars on teaching for new faculty, encourage social and community engagement, and explore the scholarship of teaching and learning.

The National Science Foundation (NSF) supported this project for several reasons. The Division of Undergraduate Education awarded the grant, with an ultimate aim of improving undergraduate science education. Furthermore, a major NSF goal is to better balance research and education in the sciences, mathematics, and engineering (NSF 1996), and it saw PFF as one way of re-balancing these roles among faculty. NSF also sought to broaden the participation of underrepresented groups with respect to gender, race, ethnicity, and disability in science and mathematics. In addition, NSF wanted to encourage disciplinary societies to take more responsibility for teaching and academic citizenship roles of faculty and to develop better balance in their own programming between research and education.

A fourth phase of PFF, funded by The Atlantic Philanthropies, was undertaken to work with disciplinary societies in the social sciences and humanities. The structure of the project is similar to that of the third phase; societies in communication, English, history, political science, psychology, and sociology are supporting the development of model PFF programs in their fields. A report on phase four will be published in late 2002.

What Did the Disciplinary Societies Do?

Each of the societies conducted a national competition in spring 1999 to award academic departments in their fields matching grants to create model PFF programs. In addition, they provided technical assistance to those departments, assisted with the assessment of these innovative programs, highlighted PFF programs in their regular meetings and publications, and generally promoted PFF as a beneficial way to educate future faculty in their disciplines. The national PFF office coordinated activities on these initiatives among the disciplinary societies and also served as the surrogate disciplinary society for the four life sciences clusters that became involved in PFF.

A total of nineteen academic departments were selected to participate in this project: five in chemistry, four each in biological and life sciences, mathematics, and physics, and two in computer science. The departments and the name of a contact person for each are listed in Appendix II. Each department organized a cluster of departments in its discipline, and each cluster, by design, represents the variety of higher education institutions likely to hire new faculty. A total of eight departments were located on campuses with existing university-wide PFF programs, and eleven were on campuses without a centralized program. Although science and mathematics faculty and graduate students had been involved in two earlier PFF projects—PFF phases one and two— this volume is based largely on the experiences of these societies and the departmental clusters with which they worked during phase three.

NSF also sought to broaden the participation of underrepresented groups.

During phases one and two, graduate deans took various steps to engage graduate faculty and to secure a sense of departmental ownership for PFF. They identified certain departments as loci for creating PFF programs, recruited key faculty to participate, and obtained departmental approval for students to participate. In phase three we reversed the process by having disciplinary societies name faculty members as principal investigators. The principal investigators worked to involve their departmental colleagues and gain the support of graduate and academic deans. To this end we required a letter of support from university administrators as part of the application process.

Table 2. Distribution of institutions participating in phase three PFF by discipline					
Type of Institution	Chemistry	Physics	Computer science	Mathe-matics	Biology/Life Sciences	TOTAL
Doctoral	5	13	2	5	4	29
Masters	7	5	4	6	11	33
Baccalaureate	15	2	3	3	6	29
Associate	5	5	0	3	5	18
Specialized	0	1	0	0	1	2
TOTAL	32	26	9	17	27	111

We also required the university to match grant funds, suggesting that funds might come in part from the offices of the graduate or academic deans. If the university had a centralized PFF program, we urged departments to take advantage of these resources as well, in the belief that doctoral education works best when the department, the university, and other institutional partners work together to support a broader education for doctoral students.

Table 2 summarizes the types of colleges and universities participating in this third phase of PFF. Across all disciplines, 74 percent of the institutions were non-doctoral granting, which nearly mirrors the fact that 64 percent of the faculty in higher education are employed at non-doctoral institutions (American Council on Education 2001). The clusters reflect the rich diversity of American higher education, and they expose graduate students to quite different institutional missions, histories, campus cultures, and student bodies—and hence, different expectations for faculty.

How Do PFF Programs Operate?

Campus leaders have been encouraged to develop PFF programs that are both in keeping with PFF concepts and reflect their particular needs, interests, and circumstances. PFF programs concentrate activities in three different loci: the university, because some learning is general and appropriate for all PFF students; the department, because some learning is particular to the disciplines; and the partner institution, because some learning is dependent on the institutional context.

Typical activities at the *university* level include a course on the general topic of college teaching and learning, forums on faculty life and careers, discussions of faculty governance issues, and development of professional portfolios documenting student expertise in teaching, research, and service.

Departments typically offer a course on the teaching of their discipline, provide sequences of supervised teaching experiences, host discussions in which faculty members from different institutions describe their careers, and sponsor talks by alumni in which they discuss how their graduate programs did and did not adequately prepare them for their jobs.

Partner institutions often assign a teaching mentor to work with doctoral students, invite students to attend department or faculty meetings, include them in faculty development activities, and offer supervised teaching opportunities.

The specific kinds of program elements developed by the science and mathematics departments in this project are discussed in Chapter 3.

What Lessons Have Been Learned From the PFF Initiative?

Numerous assessments have been conducted since PFF programs began. Here is a brief summary of the major lessons learned.

▲ PFF programs do function largely as they were conceived.

▲ Doctoral students and alumni are enthusiastic about the benefits of their PFF programs.

▲ Faculty members from partner institutions enjoy working with doctoral students and derive benefits for their own professional development.

▲ Graduate faculty members learn about faculty life in different institutions and appreciate the professional development their students receive through PFF programs.

▲ Virtually everyone involved in PFF programs says that they would recommend them to others.

▲ Benefits to academic departments and universities include better recruitment and placement of graduate students.

▲ These benefits outweigh the modest investments of time and money that are required.

Chapter 2

Strategies for Establishing a PFF Program

The hallmarks of a PFF program include institutional collaboration within a cluster, new forms of mentoring, departmental and university activities, and partner institution activities. Participants in this third phase tested the PFF ideas in practice and assessed the results. In this chapter we identify steps they took and issues they considered in establishing departmental programs.

The major impetus for PFF programs that are the focus of this report came largely from departmental faculty members, including chairs, directors of graduate studies, and faculty leaders. Graduate deans and directors of teaching-learning centers also contributed to the development of PFF programs in science and mathematics departments. A PFF program can be initiated by anyone who a) has standing in graduate education, b) is aware of the advantages offered by PFF programs, and c) is willing to work with various constituencies to forge a coalition to support experimentation with new approaches to graduate education.

The planners of this PFF project knew that educational programs established with the aid of grants often disappeared when the grant ended. They urged cluster leaders to employ strategies in developing PFF programs that would enhance their chances of being sustained beyond the conclusion of the grant period. Of course, after only three years of experience with the clusters, it is not possible to know how many of the programs will survive. But planning for sustainability is a useful approach for individuals starting new programs.

Identify a Faculty Director

Leadership by faculty members committed to innovate with core PFF concepts is pivotal to success. A faculty member who sees value in the ideals of PFF must come forward, or be recruited, to provide leadership for launching a PFF program and to serve as the director. Directors included individuals who offer a course on the teaching of the discipline, such as Arlene Russell in chemistry at the University of California, Los Angeles; senior faculty members, such as John Cumalat in physics at the University of Colorado; relatively new faculty members appointed specifically for this initiative, such as Paula Lemons in biology at Duke University; and those responsible for teaching assistant development programs, such as Virginia Warfield in mathematics at the University of Washington.

Leaders of departmental PFF programs ... need institutional support.

Effective departmental leaders need more than commitment to the PFF vision. They must be able to communicate its importance to a range of audiences, help a planning group reach agreement about a sound program design, see that the program elements are implemented, serve as mentors to the graduate student participants, and facilitate interactions between all parties involved.

Leaders of departmental PFF programs agree that if PFF directors are to be effective, more than personal qualities are needed. They also need institutional support. The leaders conclude that those who hold the assignment of PFF director as part of their regular workload have been more effective than those who, despite admirable enthusiasm, have attempted to provide leadership in addition to their normal workload. Explicit recognition of the important responsibilities of the program director by the institution—in the form of reassigned time or salary supplement—is a key element of a viable program.

Gain Graduate Faculty Participation

Graduate faculty members participate in a PFF program in a number of ways. They serve as mentors to PFF graduate students in developing their skills in teaching, research, and professional service; advise students on other aspects of the academic profession; participate in PFF seminars and workshops; and offer suggestions for improving the program and involving individuals from underrepresented groups. They often facilitate interactions between partner institution faculty and graduate students. Most discuss faculty roles with their students and encourage those who might be interested in academic careers to get involved in the PFF program.

Graduate faculty often have two concerns about PFF. Since the primary interests of most graduate faculty members are their research and the training of their students to conduct research, they are concerned that PFF might take time away from research. Their support for student participation in PFF activities depends on their understanding that research remains central to the doctoral degree and that PFF activities can be arranged so that they do not diminish students' research efforts.

Another concern of faculty is that student involvement in such a program might extend time to degree. This is a legitimate concern and needs to be addressed with accurate information. In a survey of forty-two graduate faculty involved in this project, 88 percent said they thought their students' involvement in PFF would have no significant impact on the time to degree (Thomas 2002). These results are similar to earlier surveys of graduate students (Pruitt-Logan, Gaff, and Weibl 1998), in which 83 percent said that their involvement in PFF would not increase their time to degree while 14 percent said it would. The surveys by Pruitt-Logan, et al. also found that 4 percent of students said participation would speed up the completion of the degree, possibly because they were more definite about wanting an academic career and became more goal oriented in their studies.

Caution must be used in interpreting these self-reported results offered by faculty members and students before the degrees actually were completed. Nonetheless, the majority of faculty members in the sciences and graduate students in all fields do not perceive that participation in PFF programs increases the time needed to earn a degree. Further, some students say they are not concerned that more time might be required, as long as they are learning valuable lessons that will enhance their careers.

Funding by NSF provides a powerful signal to the institutions, departments, and faculty of both the national importance of the project and its importance to the mission of the disciplines. Faculty perception of the importance of PFF is reinforced by association with their disciplinary society, and by the sponsorship provided by the national associations, the Council of Graduate Schools, and the Association of American Colleges and Universities. Similarly, institutional support for the campus program, such as matching funds or formal incorporation of PFF activities into graduate curricula, indicates that the university values PFF.

Participation in PFF events gives faculty members information about the actual program, provides them a chance to hear what their colleagues think about it, and allows them to observe that their students value PFF.

PFF leaders in science and mathematics report that most graduate faculty members who have been asked by the program director to make a short time commitment, such as participating in a panel discussion, seminar, or workshop, have been generous with their time, expertise, and facilities. Once involved, they tend to become supportive of PFF for their students. In general, less involved graduate faculty provide little active resistance to the participation of their graduate students in PFF activities, as long as these activities do not interfere with their students' research.

Identify Cluster Partners

The task of creating a cluster of different kinds of institutions—a PFF hallmark—is challenging. The cluster of diverse institutions—such as liberal arts colleges, comprehensive universities, and community colleges—represents the variety of institutional contexts within which graduate students might pursue a career. Developing this new form of institutional collaboration may involve overcoming a history of competition and stereotypes about other types of institutions and developing a spirit of cooperation for the purpose of preparing the next generation of faculty members. For example, faculty members may think in terms of prestige, making assumptions about what others might, or might not, be able to contribute to the program. And those at one institution may think of themselves as more accomplished researchers, more dedicated teachers, or more committed to educating a diverse student body than faculty at other institutions. But when faculty members collaborate and get to know each other, they soon learn that these views are simplistic, that the common hierarchies by which institutions are ranked are counterproductive, and that there are many strengths that faculty at each type of institution can bring to the program.

Issues in organizing clusters include the administrative complexity and the corresponding time required in recruiting, organizing, and maintaining the clusters. When a university already has established a centralized PFF program (as occurred with institutions that participated in the first two PFF phases), the task of organizing a departmental cluster may be a relatively easy matter, since the PFF director can take advantage of cluster arrangements already developed by the graduate school. For example, Arizona State University and the University of Washington had established PFF clusters in the first phases, before this PFF phase 3 project was initiated, so that when the departments of mathematics wished to create their own PFF programs, they could build on those continuing relationships with partner institutions. On the other hand, the departments of mathematics at Binghamton University and Virginia Polytechnic Institute and State University (Virginia Tech) were the first to initiate PFF programs at their institutions. This meant that their departmental leaders had to contact colleagues in mathematics departments at other institutions and invite them to participate in a grant application and the subsequent PFF program.

One of the challenges in the cluster concept is to explain what PFF and the anchor institution have to offer to the partner faculty, departments, and institutions.

One of the challenges in the cluster concept is to explain what PFF and the anchor institution have to offer the partner faculty, departments, and institutions. This should be carefully considered before any contact is made, since partner school representatives often ask this question early in discussions about setting up a cluster.

A number of relationships already may exist between research universities and potential partner institutions, including research and educational collaborations between faculty members and administrators; these relationships can be the starting point for developing clusters. Once potential partner faculty are identified, the next step in their recruitment is to invite them to an initial meeting where the goals are explained and program possibilities are presented. After they have become involved in the program, they can be asked to recruit some of their colleagues.

Appoint a Steering Committee

It is necessary to involve all the relevant constituencies from participating institutions in the process of defining program goals, planning program activities, and developing long-range plans. That is why PFF leaders in science and mathematics recommend forming a steering committee that includes graduate faculty members, graduate students, and graduate or academic deans, as well as faculty members and academic administrators from partner institutions. Ideally, as with the physics cluster at the University of California, San Diego, the steering committee includes a staff member from the graduate university's center for teaching and learning, which has resources that can be a source of support for the PFF program.

The committee usually needs to take time to assess members' perspectives on preparation of future faculty, understand differences in their academic cultures, and sense the potential contributions that each institution can make to the cluster. Meetings that include a meal or refreshments usually improve attendance and provide a comfortable context for discussions.

Once the PFF program has begun, leaders have found it valuable for the steering committee to shift its focus from planning to overseeing the program. They suggest that the committee meet at least once per academic term to keep participants informed about program events and to discuss issues related to the program. Continuing opportunities for communicating across constituencies and reaffirming involvement are critical to an effective program. In order to facilitate communication, each partner institution usually has one designated contact who is familiar with the overall PFF program.

Many programs appoint a senior graduate student as PFF administrative assistant, which is itself a valuable experience, because this assistant is at the hub of program planning and administration and sees the program from the perspectives of all constituencies. Communication among participants is vital, and some programs facilitate this by developing a PFF cluster Web site or electronic listserv.

Recruit Graduate Student Participants

Graduate students have a hunger for professional development opportunities concerning academic careers, and they tend to be attracted to the ideas of PFF. Their recruitment is among the easiest tasks in setting up a program. Indeed, graduate students are perhaps the best advocates for PFF and the best recruiters, often through informal conversations with their peers. Just as in marketing products, word of mouth seems to be the best advertising for PFF.

Graduate students are attracted to PFF for a variety of reasons. Some are certain they want an academic career and seek to learn as much as they can about their chosen profession. Others want to explore the possibility of a faculty career and wish to learn about faculty roles at a variety of institutions.

Many say that they would like to enhance their teaching capacities and acquire credentials. Nearly all want to be more competitive in securing their first academic position, and they believe that PFF gives them both some valuable experience that others may not have and a "credential" that constitutes a competitive advantage.

One of the critical recruitment issues is that women, African Americans, Hispanics, and persons with disabilities are underrepresented in the sciences and mathematics. PFF leaders have sought to enhance the participation of underrepresented groups by connecting recruitment efforts to institutional programs designed to facilitate the matriculation of members of these groups. One example is the biology PFF program at the University of South Carolina, which builds on the institution's ongoing efforts to encourage minority graduate students to pursue careers in academia through its African American Professors Program. Another example is the Howard University program in physics, which draws minority students through the university's Alliances for Graduate Education and the Professoriate program (AGEP).

Graduate students are perhaps the best advocates for PFF and the best recruiters.

PFF leaders report that the flexibility of their programs enables graduate students to participate when they are interested and for as long as their interest and time allow. Some graduate students find that during their first two years, PFF programs complement teaching assistant training and improve their contribution to the department's undergraduate teaching efforts. Those in their later years may benefit more from participating in intensive teaching activities at cluster institutions, such as co-teaching a course, or a portion of a course, with a mentor at the cluster institution or being responsible for an entire course during the summer or regular academic year. Students in the later stages of their graduate work also benefit from participating in service activities, such as faculty governance and community engagement.

Several PFF programs offer their participants graduate credit for courses, some give a certificate for completion, and others note PFF participation on the transcript. However it is done, recognition for student completion of a PFF program is important. The addition of a formally documented PFF experience on the résumé and transcript can significantly improve a graduate student's chances of obtaining an academic position at those institutions that consider good teaching and service to be important criteria in new faculty hires. Documentation also helps to create a market demand for this new type of faculty preparation by informing faculty search committees about candidates with special qualifications.

Institute New Forms of Mentoring

Mentoring is another hallmark of PFF programs. It takes several forms: both traditional mentoring for research by graduate faculty and mentoring for teaching and professional service by both graduate and partner faculty. The relationship between graduate students and their dissertation research mentors is usually well defined. The PFF mentoring relationship typically is more flexible and is designed to meet the particular professional development needs of the graduate student. An important advantage of the PFF program is that participating students have access to at least one mentor other than the research adviser. This allows students to establish a relationship with faculty members who have expertise in their content specialties as well as expertise in teaching and service.

One of the most powerful innovations of PFF is the opportunity for graduate students to work with a faculty mentor at a partner institution. This arrangement offers graduate students a relationship with faculty members who can introduce them to the distinctive qualities of the partner institution, the specific challenges of teaching that institution's student body, and the roles of faculty members in the shared governance of their department or institution.

The process of assigning PFF mentors to students varies. Some directors collect résumés from faculty and allow graduate students to choose mentors, or vice versa. Often the assignment results from a stepwise process of exchanging information between both parties until a decision is made. Sometimes graduate students visit a partner institution and meet with potential mentors. Mentoring begins when a suitable relationship with one of those faculty is agreed to.

Regardless of how the relationship is established, PFF leaders agree that it is important for both parties to decide on a specific set of goals, activities, means of assessment and feedback, and the amount of time involved. Truman Schwartz, a professor from Macalester College, and Sherri Hunt, a chemistry student at the University of Minnesota, were a mentor-mentee pair. They identified five keys to a successful PFF mentoring experience (Hunt and Schwartz 2001): thorough preparation, good communication, clear goals, significant effort by both mentor and mentored student, and compatible personalities.

In the PFF program in biology at the University of South Carolina, graduate students who serve as adjunct instructors at a partner school are assigned to a faculty mentor. The goal is for the student to develop a sustained relationship with at least one faculty mentor who can not only reveal some of the mysteries of the academy but also serve as a professional colleague. Often, this mentor later serves as a reference in the job search and becomes part of a professional network when the student becomes a new faculty member.

The goal is for the student to develop a sustained relationship with at least one faculty mentor who can not only reveal some of the mysteries of the academy but also serve as a professional colleague.

PFF leaders indicate that the mentoring relationship usually has positive outcomes for both graduate students and faculty. Graduate students gain insights and perspectives from their mentors. For example, Jason Cody, an assistant professor of chemistry at Lake Forest College (Cody 2001), said that his PFF experience while at Northwestern University had considerable impact with little time invested, which he estimated was less than 100 hours, including travel. He reported three important benefits: complete responsibility for part of a course, opportunity to receive feedback on teaching without negative professional consequences, and realistic ideas about an academic career. He noted, "These benefits cannot be achieved as a TA at Northwestern." It is significant that he has since served as a faculty mentor for a PFF graduate student at his alma mater, giving back value that he received as a graduate student.

Secure the Support of Partner Faculty

Partner faculty roles are essential in PFF programs. Although their involvement varies among programs, typical activities include the following: serving as mentors to PFF students who teach units of their courses, introducing students to significant efforts on their own campuses to improve undergraduate learning, serving as participants in teaching PFF seminars, and allowing PFF students to shadow them in service activities, such as attending faculty committee meetings or participating in faculty development activities.

Responsibilities like these require the active involvement of partner institution faculty members in academic programs at research universities. When first hearing about PFF, they, like the graduate faculty, have concerns. Given the historical separation between their own institutions and the doctoral university anchoring the PFF cluster, many are suspicious that in becoming teaching mentors for graduate students, they are making up for the neglect of teaching by the graduate faculty. Frequently, they already have a heavy teaching load as well as research and service responsibilities and are concerned about taking on more work. And, it is not always clear what benefits they will derive from involvement. They want to know if they will be compensated.

Many answers to these questions are available. A precondition for a successful, ongoing PFF program is respect for the partner faculty members, their institutions, and their contributions to the education of graduate students. PFF is not a matter of compensating for deficiencies at the research university; rather, each type of institution contributes what it does best, and they collaborate so that students receive the best that each can offer.

Partner faculty members do have full-time commitments, and they do need incentives for taking on additional responsibilities. Although some PFF programs provide modest honoraria to partner faculty, most do not.

Common incentives include: provision of a small professional development fund that can be used tax-free for a variety of activities; access to the university's facilities, such as the library, laboratories, and computing resources; inclusion of the names of faculty members in printed materials and other public acknowledgment of their contributions; a formal letter of appreciation from the PFF program director, with copies to the partner institution's administration that can be used in personnel reviews; support for travel to make PFF presentations; and invitations to the department's intellectual and social activities.

Importantly, the primary motivations of partner faculty for participating in PFF programs have little to do with these tangible benefits. Most do it for a variety of intrinsic motivations. They emphatically agree that serving as mentors to PFF doctoral students is a better way of preparing the next generation of academics than the way they were prepared. Many note that they are committed to helping future faculty both see the attraction of their kind of institution and prepare for a career there. Since most of the mentors are senior faculty, they report being motivated by a disposition for generativity, for assisting the next generation in "learning the ropes" of the academic profession.

Once the goals and philosophy of PFF are understood and a spirit of mutual respect and collaboration is established, the level of acceptance of PFF at partner institutions typically is high. Partner faculty share the belief with graduate faculty that providing PFF opportunities to graduate students is the right thing to do. They also view the opportunity to interact and work with PFF participants as a major benefit. Moreover, they themselves benefit from a closer relationship with the academic department at the research university, which sometimes leads to collaboration on other professional projects.

Some partner schools that depend on a number of adjunct faculty members regard PFF programs as reliable sources of motivated and effective instructors. These schools sometimes recruit PFF students as adjunct faculty to serve as sabbatical replacements or offer courses in subjects not currently available at the partner institution. Some PFF students give talks to enrich the partner institution's program, and they can provide links to laboratories at the research university, opening new opportunities for the partner schools' undergraduates.

Secure Funding

Leaders of PFF programs, whether departmental or university-wide, understand that establishing and maintaining a program does not take a lot of money, but it does take some. Providing budgetary support is one of the key indicators that a program can be sustained after it is launched with a grant.

The grants to departments in this third phase of PFF were small—$10,000 for each of two years—and they were matched by institutional funds, giving each department a program fund of $20,000 per year. The matching funds came from various sources—the department, the graduate school, and the academic dean's office. In fact, most PFF programs did not spend the full budget after two years and were able to extend the funds to cover nearly three academic years. The fact that two large budget items—faculty salaries and student stipends—were not grant supported meant that all grant funds could be used for program purposes.

At a PFF meeting in October 2001, as the United States was in a recession, most PFF cluster leaders anticipated a continuation of PFF after the grant period. A few from states projecting reduced revenues and smaller budgets for higher education expressed concerns that budget cuts would make it difficult for their universities to support even a successful PFF program. But since budgets always reflect values and priorities, building a coalition of students and faculty members who know first hand the benefits of PFF can counteract this threat.

Departments varied in their use of the strategies identified in this chapter, and PFF leaders report that they make adjustments throughout the course of their programs so that they meet the needs of their various constituencies. From the outset the aim has been that PFF programs become institutionalized, not simply temporary additions to doctoral programs. After only three years it is not possible to know whether all the programs described in this chapter will become institutionalized, but the suggestions offered here are valuable steps toward the goal of developing sustainable programs.

Chapter 3

Content of PFF Programs in the Sciences and Mathematics

No two PFF programs are exactly alike. Faculty members design their offerings based on the distinctiveness of the discipline and their departments. Yet all focus on core PFF concepts, providing the next generation of faculty members with exposure to a broad range of experiences and settings that will better prepare them for their careers. This chapter examines nine common kinds of PFF activities: courses for credit, seminars and workshops, certificate programs, activities at partner institutions, mentoring programs, assessment and evaluation tools, attention to diversity, informal student activities, and activities and resources through the disciplinary societies.

Courses for Credit

Courses are the primary way education is organized, and this is true for PFF. The PFF program in biology at the University of Cincinnati offers three seminar courses for graduate credit. "Becoming a More Effective Teacher" and "The Academic Job Search Process" are offered through the graduate school and open to graduate students in all disciplines. They cover topics related to the job search process, the diversity of academic positions available, trends in higher education, and approaches to cultivating student learning. The third course, "Effective Tools for Teaching in the Biological Sciences," is targeted to the particular challenges and opportunities of teaching in the discipline. It includes topics such as course preparation, classroom presentation and evaluation, learning styles, technology in the classroom, and assessment. Course descriptions are available at www.uc.edu/pffls/FAQ.html. The program is open to all pre- and post-doctoral students in life sciences, including those in basic science departments and in the college of medicine.

The physics department at the University of Arkansas developed "The Internship in Higher Education Leadership" as a formal, graduate-level physics course that counts as an elective toward a physics master's or doctoral degree. The course integrates professional experience with theory and was developed in collaboration with administrators at the institutions that provide the internship experience—Crowder College, Kansas State University, and Northwest Arkansas Community College. This is a useful illustration of a goal-driven teaching apprenticeship course, described at www.uark.edu/depts/physinfo/pfpf/547v.html.

Seminars and Workshops

Less formal than courses, seminars and workshops offer exposure to teaching and learning concepts, information about job search strategies, and discussions about faculty life. Programs on pedagogy provided by university centers on teaching and learning and graduate school programs on faculty roles and responsibilities are useful resources for departmental PFF programs. Information about job search strategies and details of faculty life is often specific to schools or departments and is best provided at that level.

Binghamton University PFF alumnus William Hooper provides a participant's view of the PFF program in mathematics:

Several times a semester, a faculty member from another college (frequently one which we visited with the speaker series) would come to

Binghamton to give either a seminar talk or a workshop. These presentations ranged from an explanation of the life of a new faculty member to exposure to the use of technology in improving teaching methods. These presentations were all beneficial, and reinforced the concept of teaching as a group effort, not an individual one.

A biochemistry student in the PFF program in chemistry at Queens College said of the PFF workshops:

Several of these workshops were particularly valuable to me. Those would include the daylong seminar that covered a number of topics including new teaching techniques in chemistry and how to apply for and write a grant. At another meeting, a faculty member from Manhattan College spoke to us about her career path. She included the application, interview, and tenure process. In addition she was a former Queens College graduate student, which made her experiences really hit home. I didn't quite realize how helpful the information I obtained through PFF was until I began to go on interviews myself.... I left each PFF meeting feeling more focused on my career, and I also felt that my concerns as a graduate student mattered.

Queens College students also made special note of the value of a series of talks called "Pathways to the Professoriate," where graduate faculty informally discussed the paths they had followed to their present faculty positions. The students expressed amazement at the variety of routes that faculty members described and inevitably had many questions for each speaker. Personalizing the account of each faculty member's history has a way of "demythologizing" the process of becoming a faculty member.

Another important activity sponsored by the PFF program at Queens College was an all-day summer retreat held off-campus to focus discussion on several workshop topics. The retreat allowed the participants to discuss important topics in depth and, the director noted, enabled the students and faculty involved in PFF to reach a point of greater focus and unusually meaningful communication.

Certificate Programs

Several PFF programs in the sciences and mathematics have developed certificate programs as a means of recognizing student achievements. Certificate programs offer the opportunity to earn a formal credential that is included in a student's permanent file.

Certificate programs offer the opportunity to earn a formal credential that is included in a student's permanent file.

Duke University's Teaching Certificate in Biology program includes a course on teaching and learning, an opportunity to teach with supervision and feedback, and a mentored faculty experience. Students prepare a teaching portfolio containing a reflective essay, a statement of teaching philosophy, samples of course materials they have developed, syllabi of courses taught, and teaching evaluations. One alumna of the program says, " My participation in PFF broadened my education at Duke beyond focused lab experiments and classes by providing a forum to discuss education beyond basic research. PFF enabled me to cultivate skills that may not have developed within the framework of the traditional graduate school experience."

Opportunities for teaching and mentoring experiences are available at Duke, Durham Technical Community College, Elon University, Guilford College, and Meredith College. Another student who participated in this program describes its value: "I am pursuing the teaching certificate because I have been lucky enough to receive a research fellowship, but that fellowship necessarily limits the amount of teaching that I have done. By pursuing the certificate, I can bolster my teaching credentials in spite of that limitation."

The University of Cincinnati offers certificates from the biological sciences and the university-wide PFF programs to students who take the three seminar courses described earlier and complete a mentoring experience of at least forty hours at one of four local partner institutions. (Names of institutions associated with each cluster can be found in Appendix II. A fuller description may be found at www.uc.edu/pffls.)

The University of South Carolina has a PFF credential with set requirements that cover teaching, research, and service activities. The core requirements include attendance at teaching seminars, mentored teaching experiences with someone who is not the research adviser, mentoring undergraduate student research, and serving on the PFF steering committee. The program began with doctoral students in biology and marine science and has since expanded to include all the doctoral programs in the College of Science and Mathematics: biology, chemistry and biochemistry, geology, marine science, physics and astronomy, mathematics, and statistics.

The PFF program in physics at the University of California, San Diego, based in the university's Center for Teaching Development (CTD), established detailed competency-based criteria for gaining the CTD Certificate in College and University Teaching. To earn the certificate, participants must demonstrate competency in four areas: 1) course development, including curriculum and syllabus design; 2) effective implementation of a course they design as part of the first competency area; 3) professional roles and responsibilities of faculty; and 4) proficiency in utilizing instructional technology. Descriptions for all four competencies can be found at www.ctd.ucsd.edu/programs/pfpf/activities.htm

Activities at Partner Institutions

Several PFF programs have developed options other than a formal teaching internship program that offer PFF participants alternative ways to forge connections with undergraduates at partner institutions. For example, each semester the PFF mathematics program at Binghamton University sponsors visits to each of its partner institutions with graduate students frequently giving talks to undergraduates on topics in mathematics. PFF alumnus Zoran Sunik describes some of the benefits of these visits:

> [T]he best part of the program is the opportunity to go to the partner institutions, take a look at different departments and feel the atmosphere from the faculty point of view. It is impossible to get a similar "insider look" in one's own department, since the relations between graduate students and the faculty are already established on different premises. As part of such a visit to [SUNY College at] Oneonta, I prepared a talk, suitable for undergraduates, that I later gave during my job interview (and was offered the job).

At Virginia Tech, PFF participants in the mathematics department give talks on their research in undergraduate seminars during daylong visits to their partner institutions. These visits are viewed as ways to enhance graduate students' communication skills and job prospects, recruit new graduate students from the partner institutions to Virginia Tech, and provide partner institutions with interesting and informative speakers.

At King's College, three PFF alumni from Binghamton University's mathematics program are now members of the faculty. Alumna Denise Reboli talks about the values to partner faculty of participating in the program:

These [PFF participant-led] discussions are important to me as a member of the faculty at a partner school because I have been able to stay in touch with the trends in graduate education. This has given me additional background that I can use when I advise my students who are considering graduate school. Some of these conversations [with PFF participants] provide an opportunity to meet graduate students who will be colleagues, possibly in my own department, in the near future. Understanding what being a faculty member entails in terms of not only teaching and research, but also service, helps the graduate students know what will be expected of them when they start a full-time position.

At Howard University, PFF Fellows serve as interns at partner institutions. Chanda Macias, a doctoral student in biology, comments on the experience (Bogle 2001):

I had reservations about my internship because of the differences in mission between Catholic University and Howard University, an Historically

Black College and University. Prior to my internship I was assigned a mentor, Dr. Greene [in the department of biology at Catholic University] who was to guide me. The experience was priceless. I was inspired to open my horizons to teaching and learning environments, as well as to embrace academia with such vibrancy.

PFF physics students at the University of California, San Diego, and education staff at the Reuben H. Fleet Science Center at San Diego City College, jointly offer a unique electronics and magnetism workshop-based course that teaches the physics underpinning various exhibits at the Center. Undergraduate students in the course engage in individual projects to develop deeper understanding of the physics of one or more exhibits and give oral and written reports on their project results.

Mentoring Programs

Mentoring experiences provided within PFF programs have pleasantly surprised both faculty mentors and student participants. Neither group anticipated the level of personal and professional enrichment that students would experience or the range of personal interactions that developed. One graduate student commented, "The bonding between PFF students and between PFF students with faculty members has developed. The emotional aspect is very important for one's self image."

Binghamton University PFF alumnus William Hooper commented:

Through the mentoring program, each graduate student in the PFF program is paired with one of Binghamton University's faculty. This pairing gives the student an adviser who is as important to developing as a teacher as the student's thesis advisor is to developing as a researcher. The peer-review program then allows the students to observe each other teach and share what they have learned from their mentors. After experiencing this program, several of us found it so helpful that we began a seminar for first-year students in an attempt to pass on what we had learned.

As an integral part of its PFF program in mathematics, Virginia Tech has assigned two senior graduate teaching assistants to act as peer mentors to other graduate student teaching assistants. As a result of this program, graduate students are strongly supported and supervised in their role as teachers, resulting in increased confidence, decreased anxiety, and fewer undergraduate complaints.

Assessment and Evaluation Tools

Assessment is a powerful learning tool when it is viewed as a way to identify areas for improvement. The University of California, San Diego's Preparing Future Physics Faculty (PFPF) program uses three self-assessment modules for its fellows, one module each for pre-training, pre-internship and post-internship. These modules are included on the PFPF Web page: www-ctd. ucsd.edu/PFPF/index.html.

Binghamton University conducted a survey of PFF participants to assess how they felt PFF had influenced their preparation to deal with seven aspects of faculty life: faculty roles beyond teaching and research, differences between institutions, teaching diverse students, undergraduate research, advising students, balancing teaching and research, and using technology in the classroom. Initial results showed that thirteen of fourteen graduate students indicated they felt ill-prepared to conduct research projects with undergraduates, and the majority said they did not have adequate knowledge or experience using technology in the classroom. Subsequent activities emphasized these areas. Results of the surveys and reports are online at www.math.binghamton.edu/pff/.

Attention to Diversity

Attention to diversity—a critical element in any PFF program—takes several forms in PFF programs in the sciences and mathematics, including broadening access to underrepresented groups, supportive activities that have an impact on retention and graduation, and teaching for inclusiveness.

Several departments and universities connect their PFF programs to initiatives that attract students from underrepresented groups to graduate education. Howard University links its NSF-funded Alliances for Graduate Education and the Professoriate (AGEP) programs to the PFF program by requiring AGEP students to participate in PFF. The AGEP program is intended to increase significantly the number of students receiving doctoral degrees in the sciences, technology, engineering, and mathematics, with special emphasis on those population groups underrepresented in these fields. The Howard arrangement provides opportunities for undergraduates from minority-serving institutions to enhance their understanding of science and mathematics environments in the academy.

The physics PFF program at the University of Colorado at Boulder connects with its Graduate Assistance in Areas of National Need (GAANN) program funded by the U.S. Department of Education. Applicants for GAANN grants must set forth policies and procedures to ensure that they will seek talented students from traditionally underrepresented groups. The Colorado physics program also connects with the NSF-funded Integrative Graduate Education and Research Training (IGERT) program. IGERT was created to meet the challenges of educating Ph.D. scientists and engineers with the multidisciplinary backgrounds and the technical, professional, and personal skills needed for the career development demands of the future. It aims to facilitate greater diversity in student participation and preparation and to contribute to the development of a diverse and globally aware science and engineering workforce. Students supported by these grants are encouraged to participate in PFF.

Attention to diversity ... takes several forms in PFF programs in the sciences and mathematics.

Similarly, the University of South Carolina has linked its PFF program in the College of Science and Mathematics to activities sponsored by its GAANN grant. Its PFF participants have given presentations to students participating in South Carolina's Louis Stokes Alliances for Minority Participation (LSAMP) program. LSAMP is a NSF-funded program designed to strengthen the preparation and increase the number of minority students who complete baccalaureates in science, technology, engineering, and mathematics fields. This objective facilitates the long-term goal of increasing the production of Ph.D.s in these fields, with an emphasis on entry into faculty positions. The South Carolina LSAMP has increased the number of minority undergraduate degrees in these fields by 75 percent since 1992.

The mathematics department at Arizona State University has introduced PFF participants to the pedagogical issues facing minorities through the Strengthening Understanding of Mathematics and Science (SUMS) Institute. One of the participants, Tamil Maldonado, a Puerto Rican student, enriched her PFF experience by attending the annual Society for Advancement of Chicanos and Native Americans in Science national conferences. She said:

> It is a wonderful activity to meet people from all sciences, math, and education areas, start making new contacts and get any kind of professional and educational information you may need. The highlight for many students was the opportunity to present their research and receive feedback from top scientists.

Later in her report, she adds:

> It is my third time coming to these meetings, and every time it has been a motivation for my educational and professional career. It is wonderful to meet excellent researchers, meet new people, and actually see their work.

The Arizona State University campus-wide PFF program—which includes students in the sciences and mathematics—incorporates activities that focus on teaching for inclusiveness. Diversity is the overarching structure that ties the program modules together, and instructional and curricular content reflects that concern. Each panelist who presents in a seminar is asked to address issues of diversity. One of its seminars is called "Teaching and Learning in the Inclusive Classroom." Among the topics included are connecting with students with disabilities, being a member of an underrepresented group in the discipline, speaking from a position of privilege in the classroom, dealing with sensitive topics, and the burden of trying to represent all members of an ethnic group.

Several institutions with large enrollments of students from underrepresented groups are members of PFF clusters. Visits to these institutions help PFF students to understand a variety of institutional missions, curricular issues, and approaches to teaching and learning. Partnering with these institutions can also serve as a source of recruits to graduate study in science and mathematics. For example, Virginia State University, an historically Black university, partners with the PFF mathematics program at Virginia Tech. Adams State College and the Community College of Denver, both of which serve large numbers of Hispanic students, partner with the University of Colorado at Boulder physics program. Howard University, a historically Black university, is a lead university in physics that partners with Bowie State University, another historically Black institution.

Informal Student Activities

At Queens College, PFF students in chemistry organized a student-only regular weekly meeting, informally known as "Happy Hour." These Happy Hour meetings became informal forums to discuss research, teaching experiences, job hunting, thesis problems, social aspects of graduate school, and a number of other relevant topics. The students developed closer collegial relationships with each other as they shared their experiences and ideas. Unexpectedly, they benefited from these conversations so much that experienced doctoral students came to serve as mentors to the more junior doctoral students.

The University of Michigan's chemistry department created a number of educational projects that were pursued by small groups of graduate students and faculty members interested in the scholarship of teaching and learning. In addition to producing significant educational products, individuals learned from each other through their informal interaction. Brett Duersch, a graduate student, observed that PFF offered a "richer" experience with increased communication and support among graduate students.

Activities and Resources through the Disciplinary Societies

The disciplinary societies, via their regional and national meetings, provide a forum for bringing educational issues in the discipline to the attention of faculty from all types of institutions. They provide a means for networking and professionalization that can and should start with graduate students and continue throughout all stages of the academic career.

The societies encouraged PFF students to actively participate in disciplinary conferences. Several of these students expressed surprise that by doing so, they gained valuable insight into effective methods for teaching in their discipline. The idea that groups of mathematicians, for example, could work together to develop and refine a pedagogically sound way to teach a course in calculus was a surprise to graduate students who had the impression that teaching was a solitary activity. PFF participants in mathematics at the University of Washington had a similar experience when they attended a local conference on the teaching of linear algebra. They also were enthusiastic about the opportunity to interact with several attendees, especially community college faculty members, because those faculty were innovative in teaching mathematics to a broad range of students.

The American Association of Physics Teachers (AAPT) reports that PFF programs help departments take seriously the importance and relevance of physics education research to the discipline. Further, the idea of seamless education from kindergarten through the baccalaureate degree is becoming part of the vocabulary of physics educators as well as of the education community in general. AAPT disseminates information about new approaches and developments in physics education through its two publications, *The Physics Teacher* magazine and *The American Journal of Physics*. In addition, the association hosts two annual meetings where workshops and presentations focus on issues of pedagogy and course content. Preparing Future Physics Faculty programs complement AAPT's vision of the future of physics education, as well as the society's other programs for the preparation of elementary and secondary teachers, the New Physics and Astronomy Faculty Workshops, and efforts focused on the revitalization of undergraduate physics.

The idea of seamless education from kindergarten through the baccalaureate degree is becoming part of the vocabulary of physics educators as well as of the education community in general.

The American Chemical Society (ACS) supports a strong program in chemical education and has a tradition of offering graduate students opportunities to develop their professional skills through presentations at meetings, which also serve as a forum for establishing contacts with individuals who will be professional colleagues. ACS views the PFF program as a logical extension of existing professional development efforts sponsored by the Society, including: The new Office of Graduate

Education (see www.acs.org/education/gradeducation.html), the *Journal of Chemical Education,* the world's premier chemical education journal (see jchemed.chem.wisc.edu/AboutJCE/index.html), and the department of career services (see Chemistry.org/portal/Chemistry?PID=acsdisplay.html and DOC=education\student\career.html).

The American Mathematical Society (AMS) and the Mathematical Association of America (MAA) have recognized the importance of sharing effective approaches to teaching and learning in undergraduate mathematics courses primarily through their meetings, workshops, and Web sites. Their meetings provide a fertile environment for reinforcing the importance of incorporating modern teaching and learning concepts. PFF programs strengthen these approaches by encouraging early, active involvement of doctoral students in association activities. Among the professional development activities organized and supported by MAA are a calendar of professional development opportunities for faculty and graduate student members, pilot programs such as the Teaching Future Teachers Pilot Workshop held after the 2002 annual meeting, workshops on grant writing, access to a teaching assistant handbook, and guidelines for programs and departments in undergraduate mathematics. MAA also maintains a teaching and learning section on its Web site (www/maa.org) that provides articles about teaching mathematics. It includes information about the MAA special interest group on research in undergraduate mathematics education, as well as Project NExT: New Experiences in Teaching, the MAA program for new faculty members interested in the teaching and learning of undergraduate mathematics.

The Association for Computing Machinery's (ACM) Special Interest Group on Computer Science Education (SIGCSE) holds an annual technical symposium to discuss education-related issues. The 2001 meeting included the session "The Nuts and Bolts of Academic Careers: A Primer for Students and Beginning Faculty." Participants addressed faculty work issues, different types of institutions and idiosyncrasies of institutions within types, and orientation for new faculty members. This session was followed by an informal Birds-of-a-Feather discussion led by current Ph.D. candidates in computer science. Also of interest at this meeting was a panel discussion on pedagogical techniques. *ACM Crossroads,* the association's electronic magazine for students, includes links to mentoring and internship opportunities, as well as articles on career development and discipline-specific topics (see www.acm.org/crossroads/resources/career.html).

Although the content among PFF programs varies from institution to institution, the kinds of program activities described in this chapter are quite common. One of the strengths of PFF is its flexibility, which allows each program to adapt to the needs of students, faculty, and the challenges of a particular discipline.

Chapter 4

Outcomes of PFF Programs

What do graduate students do in PFF programs, and how do they benefit from them? Are the outcomes the ones anticipated? Are the outcomes worth the substantial effort needed to create clusters, establish new forms of mentoring, and engage faculty members in several program components? What are the experiences and outcomes for faculty members, the departments, and the disciplinary societies?

Extensive assessment has been done on PFF, including surveys of graduate student and faculty participants by the PFF staff, case studies by program directors, surveys and interviews with PFF alumni, interviews with society leaders and graduate deans, and surveys and participant observation by commissioned expert assessors.

The results are universally positive. For example, students report that, compared to their peers, they know more about the academic profession and the variety of institutions where they may work, they know more about teaching and learning, and they are more sophisticated in their understanding of faculty roles. Partner faculty benefit from the opportunity to work with advanced graduate students, are gratified to mentor a junior colleague, gain insights from seeing another person teach a portion of their course, and feel revitalized. Graduate faculty report learning about different kinds of institutions, the changing roles of faculty, and conditions in the job market, and they appreciate the education their students receive. Almost every graduate student and faculty member who has been queried has said they would recommend PFF to others.

Views of the PFF Directors

In connection with the science and mathematics PFF project funded by NSF and the humanities and social science PFF project funded by The Atlantic Philanthropies, an independent assessment of PFF is being conducted. So far, questionnaires have been completed by sixty-five of sixty-seven PFF program directors and by thirty-three graduate deans. Questionnaires were sent to approximately 400 graduate and 450 partner faculty in spring 2002, and surveys will be sent in fall 2002 to approximately 4,000 graduate students who have participated in PFF.

Preliminary results from the surveys of directors of PFF programs and graduate deans are that 55 percent said their programs were "very successful," and 42 percent reported them to be "somewhat successful"; none of the programs in science and mathematics were judged to be "not successful." When asked what aspects of their programs contributed most to their success, the following responses were cited:

▲ "The combination of graduate students who see the need for PFF activities in their preparation and energetic faculty members who have taken the lead in providing them, is a self-motivating, self-propelling kind of synergy."

▲ "Students really like the interdisciplinary discussions and emphasis on diversity throughout our seminar series."

▲ "Our program promotes graduate student interaction, autonomy, and self-development. Individuals who emerge from the process are better able to act on and talk about their futures as scholars, teachers, and faculty members."

▲ "Our students have at least two full-fledged mentorships during PFF. Our partner faculty have been very high quality. Many of them have had students every year or even every semester for five years."

▲ "The program conveys to students that they are being prepared to be professionals in the full sense of the term."

▲ "Support from chair, graduate dean, and provost. Enthusiasm of several students involved in the program. Cooperation with partners to make this a reciprocal, mutually beneficial arrangement."

▲ "The fact that PFF activities are a formal, required part of our program, not an add-on."

As we suspected when launching this project, PFF seems to be more difficult to obtain buy-in among science and mathematics faculty than faculty in other fields. Although project directors report that graduate faculty are generally supportive of PFF, faculty support and participation in PFF is weaker in the sciences and mathematics disciplines than in the humanities and social sciences or in the university-wide programs. Although 82 percent of directors agree or somewhat agree that PFF graduate students work closely with faculty at partner institutions, the level of participation of partner institutions in PFF programs in science and mathematics was judged to be lower than for the other PFF phases. In terms of visibility for PFF in their disciplines, 82 percent of the directors said that PFF sessions at conferences or meetings had either a significant (38 percent) or limited (44 percent) impact, and 68 percent indicated that stories in society newsletters had an impact on visibility. The directors of programs in the sciences and mathematics regarded the presentations and newsletter items as producing less visibility in their societies than did those in other fields or in university-wide programs.

These findings may be the result of fewer science students planning for academic careers or the greater external funding of research that makes any departure from research more problematic in the sciences than in the other disciplines. They also suggest that additional time, strategies, and effort may be necessary to convince scientists of the value of PFF. It is important for scientists to learn from fellow scientists about their actual experiences with PFF and the benefits such programs provide for their students.

Views of Science and Mathematics Participants

The assessment report of this PFF program in science and mathematics, prepared by Veronica Thomas (Thomas 2002), contains additional details about the experiences and outcomes for participants. Thomas attended major PFF events, interviewed disciplinary society leaders, developed a series of related questionnaires for graduate students, graduate faculty, and partner faculty, sent them to cluster participants, and analyzed and summarized the results.

Thomas received 173 completed questionnaires: ninety-nine from graduate students, forty-two from graduate faculty, and thirty-two from partner faculty. Respondents were from thirteen of the nineteen clusters in this project. The results from Thomas's surveys are consistent with previous surveys with larger samples and from additional disciplines. She instructed cluster leaders who distributed the forms to include only "central participants," not individuals who may have participated in an isolated PFF activity or event.

Thomas's overall conclusion (2) is:

[T]he participants from the three key stakeholder groups (i.e., students, graduate faculty, and partner faculty) were very enthusiastic in their support of PFF, and they generally assessed the program quite positively.

The participants felt that the program had both unique and overlapping benefits for students, faculty, the graduate department, and the cluster institution.

Experiences of Graduate Students and Alumni

The doctoral students in Thomas's study were 58 percent male and 68 percent Caucasian. Twenty-nine percent were enrolled in chemistry or biochemistry programs, 22 percent in physics, 22 percent in mathematics or computer science, 21 percent in biology, and 6 percent in other science fields. The following sections summarize the aggregated survey responses.

Motives and expectations for participating. Students were asked why they decided to participate in PFF. Typical replies include the following:

▲ "I have a strong interest in science education and I decided that PFF would provide me with educational opportunities that otherwise would not be available."

▲ "I was curious to learn about liberal arts colleges" (or, in other cases, community colleges, or simply diverse institutions).

▲ "I thought it would help me decide what kind of job I wanted and prepare me for the job search."

▲ "Some day I would like a job, a job that fits my desires. PFF can be informative, a résumé builder, and help with teaching skills."

A few indicated that they had little choice, as they were "encouraged" or "asked" by a faculty member to participate, or even required by one department, which saw PFF as a way to launch a new teaching assistant development program. On the other hand, some said that their faculty were not familiar with PFF and that they learned of the opportunity only through student friends.

Ninety-five percent of the graduate students indicated that their PFF program had, to date, "met" or "exceeded" their original expectations. Given the various reasons that students are attracted to PFF programs and the early stage of the programs, this represents a positive endorsement. Student responses also compare favorably to an earlier assessment (Pruitt-Logan, Gaff, and Weibl 1998).

Most valuable activities. In her evaluation, Thomas asked about which PFF activities were most valuable (2002, 13). Among aspects that students reported *valuing the most* are: the diverse learning experiences provided by the program; new knowledge gained from PFF seminars, conferences, and discussion sessions; networking opportunities; exposure to different types of institutions; and opportunity to work more closely with faculty.

Obstacles. Evaluations of PFF programs are not all positive, and Thomas's assessment (2002, 15) inquired into the obstacles, which she summarized: "The biggest obstacles to participation in the PFF program cited by students centered around time constraints." Other concerns were logistics and travel, lack of information and orientation, difficulty finding a mentor, and lack of awareness among the department faculty. These are all problems that, once identified, can be addressed. Time constraints were the most unforgiving of the problems. Nonetheless, one student seemed to sum up the sense of the group by saying, "The information learned is definitely worth the time invested."

Outcomes. One outcome this study sought to examine was student interest in academic careers. Fifty-six percent of those surveyed reported that their interest in a career in the academy increased as a result of their participation in PFF. One person put it this way:

> I was fairly unhappy with teaching as a result of my experience as a TA. Over the course of this quarter, seeing some of the exciting things that people do in other institutions, seeing what their classes are like, and getting a feel about how the institutions worked reminded me why I had been interested in a teaching career initially. PFF was not the only reason for this change, but it certainly was influential in getting me more excited again.

Desire for an academic career remained about the same for 40 percent of students who responded, probably because so many began PFF with an interest in becoming a faculty member. Four percent reported that their desire for an academic career decreased. Although we do not know what contributed to their decreased interest, the realization that academic life was not attractive to them was an important lesson to learn at a time when they could easily make a change in their career trajectory.

Other outcomes are captured in the following student comments.

▲ "There are two aspects I have gotten out of the PFF program. The first is very practical and has included advice on résumé/CV preparation, a seminar on grant writing, etc. The second aspect, which is most important, is that as a result of the graduate students getting to know each other through PFF meetings, we have all become more interested in helping each other."

▲ "It has helped me to gain self-confidence in my abilities."

▲ "The kind of perspectives I was exposed to, I have not encountered anywhere else in the 4.5 years I have been at [this] University."

▲ "The department has a pretty narrow view of our career options. This broadens them."

▲ "I believe my generation of scientists, and even more so the students at my institution, do not have a sense of what the community they are entering is really about. I think they are curious and as a result respond well to the invitation for discussion of their future."

Recommendations. All constituencies were asked whether they would recommend their PFF program to others, and the results were nearly unanimous. Of the 166 respondents, 165 would recommend PFF. This is similar to earlier surveys (Pruitt-Logan, Gaff, and Weibl 1998) in which 99 percent of graduate students, graduate faculty, and partner faculty said they would recommend PFF. This remarkable uniformity of opinion is seldom seen in survey research.

Evidence from PFF alumni. During the three years of PFF phase 3 programs, only a few graduate students received their degrees and secured academic appointments. The following individuals credit their experience in PFF as a contributing factor in their early career success: physicist Andi Pascarella from Colorado was hired at the University of Northern Iowa; biologist Faye Grimley from Cincinnati was hired as an assistant professor with a joint appointment at Tulane University in environmental health sciences and at Xavier University in biology; mathematician Joseph Evan from Binghamton joined the faculty at King's College; chemist Jaimielee Cohen from Queens became an assistant professor at Pace University; and computer scientist James Hauser from Cincinnati was hired as an assistant professor at Northern Kentucky University.

A survey (DeNeef 2002) of PFF alumni who are in faculty positions provides further insight. The DeNeef survey included individuals not just in the sciences and mathematics but also in the social sciences and humanities. A total of 271 alumni were surveyed, of whom 129 returned completed questionnaires. Twenty-five respondents were interviewed by telephone.

DeNeef concluded that PFF made a difference in the experiences of these individuals in three primary ways. First, the alumni report that because of their involvement in PFF, they believe their graduate student experience was qualitatively different—and better—than it might have been. Second, they believe that PFF experiences aided them in their job search, with PFF typically credited as a central reason they received their job offers. Third, they report that what they learned through PFF helped them as new faculty members to get off to a faster and surer start than their faculty peers.

One of the more surprising of DeNeef's findings is that PFF alumni are serving as resources to their new faculty colleagues. For example, Wendy Crone, a new faculty member in engineering at the University of Wisconsin, Madison, reported that "PFF provided me with a basket of tools that I am still trying out, tools that I can pick and choose from as the need arises." This is a common outcome among PFF alumni, according to DeNeef. But in Crone's case, because she has this "basket of tools," her peers are seeking her advice on various professional matters. "I have become a *de facto* mentor to my colleagues," she observed (DeNeef, 16).

Faculty Members

Expectations. Thomas (2002) reports that 92 percent of the graduate science and mathematics faculty and all of the partner faculty said that their PFF program had met or exceeded their expectations. Further, the majority of graduate faculty reported strong support from their department chair and faculty colleagues. Seventy-five percent indicated that the support of the chair for PFF was positive, and 86 percent said that faculty support was positive. These perceptions differ from the students', several of whom reported that not many faculty knew about PFF or spoke favorably of it, and that they had to obtain information about PFF from other students.

Graduate faculty benefits. Graduate faculty members were asked about the benefits they derived from participating in PFF, and they gave a range of answers that have been typical since the beginning of PFF.

- ▲ "Deeper understanding of the roles and responsibilities of faculty members at various institutions, as well as enormously beneficial professional development."
- ▲ "The opportunity to get to know some students quite well; to share my ideas on teaching and to learn from them."
- ▲ "Enthusiasm of students."
- ▲ "One of my senior doctoral students has just become the first successful faculty placement from our PFF program."
- ▲ "Better understanding, communication with students involved. It also helped me to single out some glitches in our graduate program that we need to work on."

Partner faculty benefits. Partner faculty, too, reported that they derived a number of benefits similar to those in previous reports.

▲ "Great contacts, teaching ideas from the seminars I have attended, and I get reinvigorated about my own teaching."

▲ "My students benefit from hearing about topics in mathematics not included in our curriculum."

▲ "Contact with professors from other institutions."

▲ "Human resources (adjunct faculty, laboratory supervisors, etc.) for my department."

▲ "Satisfaction from helping future faculty."

Both groups of faculty reported becoming energized or revitalized by working with PFF graduate students and reconnected with the roots of their interest in an academic career.

Department Benefits. There is some evidence that academic departments also benefit from PFF. Thomas (2002) asked graduate students whether the existence of a PFF program had influenced their view of the quality of their department. Slightly over half, 55 percent, said it increased their positive regard for the department, while the remaining 45 percent indicated it had no effect.

In terms of recruiting high-quality students to the department, 55 percent of the graduate faculty reported that PFF would be "definitely useful"; the rest thought it "might be." Some students said that PFF was a factor in their choice of a graduate program, and one volunteered it was a useful recruiting device. One student in chemistry stated that "The PFF program helps us to attract better graduate [students]."

Finally, a great deal of evidence indicates that PFF develops sophisticated and savvy students who are able to navigate the job search more effectively than their peers without PFF experience. This suggests that graduates of a department with a PFF program have a competitive advantage in their initial academic job search.

Although many people say PFF is "the right thing to do," it also seems to have strategic benefits for departments that embrace it. It can strengthen the perceived quality of the department and aid in the recruitment and placement of students. Of course, additional empirical data are needed to confirm these initial observations.

Growing Recognition of PFF

Researchers of graduate education and faculty careers are beginning to recognize the power of PFF programs. Ann Austin (2002) summarized the research evidence in an article titled "Preparing the Next Generation of Faculty: Graduate School as Socialization to the Academic Career." She cites PFF as a "praiseworthy exception" to the common fact that graduate students have little exposure to different faculty cultures and expectations at different types of institutions. In a publication called *Heeding New Voices*, Eugene Rice and his colleagues (2000) interviewed over 350 graduate students and young faculty, including PFF participants. The authors called future faculty preparation programs "promising practices" that help graduate students to have realistic views of an academic career.

The evidence is far from complete, about the experiences of participants and the outcomes of PFF programs, but there is growing evidence that these programs, in general, have positive outcomes for doctoral students, graduate faculty, partner faculty, and graduate departments. That is why a brochure published by the American Association of Physics Teachers (n.d. 7) declares,

> The changes precipitated by PFF programs constitute a win-win-win strategy:

> ▲ Better preparation for the doctoral students,
> ▲ Better faculty candidates for the colleges and universities that hire them, and
> ▲ Stronger, more engaging programs for doctoral degree-granting departments.

The next chapter will examine challenges that need to be overcome if PFF programs are to be sustained and continue to be a winning strategy.

Chapter 5

Prospects for the Future

This initiative to launch Preparing Future Faculty programs in the sciences and mathematics was prompted by the need to involve more graduate faculty in bringing their doctoral programs into closer alignment with the many expectations of new faculty. The most important expectation, of course, is to provide excellent science education. It is now time to draw from what has been learned to help chart the future course for PFF.

Higher education has a long history of educational innovations emerging, gaining widespread attention, and then disappearing from the landscape, especially those dependent on external funding. A major challenge for the future of PFF is to sustain the programs. This challenge is especially problematic in science and mathematics, because programs in these disciplines have had only three years to experiment with these innovations. It is encouraging that leaders at all of the participating societies and at most of the clusters have indicated they intend to continue with their initiatives. However, three years is hardly enough time to change the "culture of preparation" in a single department, let alone within a discipline or throughout such a large, complex, and decentralized operation as doctoral education.

One of the most important forces that makes PFF timely is the much anticipated generational change taking place among college faculties. Large numbers of professors are retiring, and the academy has an historic opportunity to prepare their successors more effectively, so they can provide academic leadership for decades in the future. If PFF is to successfully respond to this opportunity, further strategic actions will be required, including:

▲ embedding within graduate education elements of professional preparation for the professoriate

▲ increasing the responsiveness of PFF to demographic changes

▲ stimulating a demand for professionally prepared faculty

▲ continuing leadership by the disciplinary societies

▲ expanding PFF to more doctoral programs

▲ linking PFF to important reforms in undergraduate education

▲ fostering professional development as a component in programs of financial support of graduate students.

Embedding within graduate education elements of professional preparation for the professoriate

A fundamental premise of professional education is that one prepares for a profession by experiencing it in the variety of settings in which it is practiced. Preparation for a number of professions takes advantage of a wide variety of internships, residencies, and fieldwork that are seldom found in preparation for the academy. Medical students, for example, work on hospital floors and in a variety of clinics early in their training, later serving as interns and residents with increased responsibilities. Some law students work in clinical courses and others work as interns in law firms or with judges practicing the legal work they aspire to do. Seminarians, while still studying toward their degrees, work in parishes and preach. These practices are more than simply experiential education, as valuable as that may be. A new doctor must know a great deal about anatomy and pharmaceuticals

but also must have experience treating patients. Similarly, it is not suffi-
cient for faculty to know only the content of their fields; they also must
understand effective teaching and advising and understand how to relate to
students as learners.

A significant body of research exists on the academic profession, which
could greatly benefit graduate students. For example, this literature discusses
effectiveness of different approaches to teaching
(McKeachie 1999; Menges, Weimer, and
Associates 1996); learning (Bransford, et al.
1999; Chickering and Gamson 1987); the curriculum (Gaff and Ratcliff 1997); assessment
(López 1999); and the impact of college on students (Astin, 1993; Pascarella and Terenzini
1991), among others. Faculty members can
learn a great deal about their professional practice from this scholarly work, which should be
used more broadly.

> *Faculty ...
> must understand
> effective teaching
> and advising
> and understand
> how to relate to
> students as learners.*

Similarly, there is a scholarly literature
about the operation of colleges and universities
and about professional concepts such as academic freedom, shared governance, and peer review, which students seldom encounter in graduate school.

Barbara Van Dresek, a graduate student in geography at the University of
Minnesota, spoke for many when she said, "Professional development for
graduate students is a subversive activity." It doesn't have to be that way.
Doctoral education should be rich in opportunities for professional development, assuredly in the conduct of research, but also in other ways that are
important to the future careers of graduate students.

Increasing the responsiveness of PFF programs to demographic changes

The demographic composition of the U.S. population poses distinct challenges for the preparation of future faculty in the sciences and mathematics. Underrepresentation can be seen in a few statistics: in 2000, 17,064 science and engineering doctoral degrees were awarded to U.S. citizens and permanent residents, but only eighty-eight doctoral degrees were awarded to American Indians, 704 to Hispanic Americans, and 728 to African Americans (NSF 2001). It is also reflected in the ranks of science and mathematics faculty. In 1999, underrepresented minorities accounted for 6.0 percent of full-time faculty in the physical sciences, 5.3 percent in mathematics, 6.0 percent in computer science, and 5.3 percent in life sciences (NSF 2002b).

A challenge for PFF programs is to recruit students from underrepresented groups. ... A second set of challenges [is] ... educating the next generation of scientists and mathematicians.

Thus, a challenge for PFF programs is to recruit students from underrepresented groups in order to produce a cohort of diverse, well-trained faculty. Several programs, such as NSF's Alliances for Graduate Education and the Professoriate (AGEP), are working to increase the numbers of underrepresented students who aspire to academic careers in the sciences and mathematics. Other programs such as NSF's Louis Stokes Alliances for Minority Participation (LSAMP) are successfully producing large increases of non-traditional students completing bachelor's degrees in sciences and mathematics. The U.S. Department of Education's Ronald E. McNair Postbaccalaureate Achievement Program prepares underrepresented groups for graduate studies through involvement in research and other scholarly activities. The Compact for Faculty Diversity is quite successful in producing minority Ph.D.s and encouraging them to seek faculty positions. Individual PFF programs need to deliberately seek partnerships with such programs to identify and attract underrepresented students. The rich resources of best practices that have been assembled by PFF programs and posted or linked through the PFF Web site can help leaders achieve their goals for participation of underrepresented groups (www.preparing-faculty.org).

A second set of challenges centers around developing in all PFF students an understanding of instructional and curricular issues involved in educating the next generation of scientists and mathematicians. Retention data from the National Science Foundation (NSF 2002c) reflect this point.

> Although approximately 25–30 percent of students entering college in the United States intend to major in S&E [science and engineering] fields, a considerable gap exists between freshman intentions and successful completion of S&E degrees. . . . The study also shows that underrepresented minorities complete S&E programs at a lower rate than other groups.

Because the increased need for highly developed scientific talent has created an emphasis on human resources, the pressure is strong to educate nontraditional students, including persons with disabilities. Instructional issues include low expectations from faculty, poor quality of teaching, and an inflexible curriculum (NSF 2000). Curriculum issues center around choices that are made about topics for study in both individual courses and degree programs, around printed and audiovisual materials, and around topics for assignments, research projects, or theses and dissertations (Chism and Pruitt 1995).

PFF programs such as the one at Arizona State University already teach aspiring faculty about the interpersonal and pedagogical approaches that should be used by faculty in effectively communicating with persons from a broad range of cultural and ethnic backgrounds. The goal is to strengthen teaching skills and overall effectiveness as educators and mentors. Clusters, such as the one anchored by the University of Colorado at Boulder, that include colleges and universities with a wide range of underrepresented groups, help to sensitize future science and mathematics faculty to these teaching and learning challenges. The need is to support and promote such partnerships.

It is clear that individual PFF programs must be much more aggressive in ensuring that they include underrepresented students as both PFF participants and as part of classroom populations that PFF participants experience.

Stimulating a demand for professionally prepared faculty

The task of enhancing the preparation of new science and mathematics faculty members is much too complex an undertaking to leave to a single initiative. To succeed, it will require strategic partnerships and alliances involving college and university senior faculty, and support from central administrators, governing bodies, and other policy makers. One example of an attempt to affect the market is a joint statement (Commonwealth Partnership 1996) by the Commonwealth Colleges of Pennsylvania, a consortium of liberal arts colleges, specifying the qualities they are seeking in new faculty. These include the very qualities PFF programs seek to develop – strengths in teaching, research, and service. Central administrators, members of governing boards, and policy makers can insist on hiring faculty who are broadly prepared in teaching, research, and service.

Similarly, faculty search committees could set higher expectations and look to candidates to provide more documentation of their professional accomplishments. A recent review of research about what colleges and universities want in new faculty (Adams 2002) identifies several common expectations: effective teaching that engages students and supports learning; a program of research suited to the circumstances and resources of the institution; and active involvement in the academic life of the campus, including shared governance. Adams makes specific recommendations to include these elements more prominently in doctoral programs. Adams also cites evidence that graduate students need more assistance with job searches and greater awareness of career options that are available in a wide variety of colleges and universities.

These kinds of actions can stimulate the market demand for more effectively prepared new faculty. If the institutions that hire faculty put a premium on PFF, that will help convince graduate departments that they should provide this training for their graduate students. It would be refreshing to see more advertisements for faculty like the one issued by the department of psychology at Occidental College in November 2001, which states explicitly, "PFF experience preferred."

Continuing leadership by disciplinary societies

The work of changing the shape of doctoral education for future professors in the sciences and mathematics needs to be continued and expanded. The disciplinary societies participating in this project have been pioneers in exploring a new approach to the preparation of future faculty, and yet there are many other disciplinary societies in science, mathematics, and engineering fields that have yet to grasp the potential of PFF. One challenge is for this initial group of societies to serve as models for other societies, and for their leaders to spread PFF ideas and programs to other fields, where some interest in PFF has already been expressed. For example, the National League for Nursing has established its Think Tank on Graduate Preparation for the Nurse Educator Role, the board endorsed a statement supporting greater attention to preparing nurse educators, and members are eager to learn of initiatives such as PFF that might guide their work.

The disciplinary societies [are] significant players in science education reform and in the national effort to improve the quality of teaching and learning.

Participation in PFF typically reinforces other educational reform initiatives at the societies, including promoting the scholarship of teaching and learning, seeking to increase access for underrepresented groups, and providing professional development opportunities for new faculty. Collectively, these kinds of activities are making the disciplinary societies significant players in science education reform and in the national effort to improve the quality of teaching and learning. James Applegate (2002, 1), past president of the National Communication Association, articulates the rationale for the leadership role of disciplinary societies in campus educational improvement agendas:

> Disciplinary societies signal what is important and define quality in their fields by the content of their journals, the programs at their conferences, and the special activities they sponsor. If it is important for the academy to do a better job preparing future faculty, creating socially engaged campuses, or embedding the scholarship of teaching and learning into campus classrooms, these agendas need to be embraced by disciplinary societies.

Expanding PFF to more doctoral programs

Although this report documents the creation of nineteen new departmental PFF programs that supplement those created in the first two phases, this is a small fraction of the total number of Ph.D. programs in the sciences and mathematics. Clearly, PFF programs are available to only a small proportion of doctoral students preparing for an academic career. As more faculty members and other leaders of doctoral programs learn about PFF programs, and as more evidence about their effectiveness develops, we may expect more institutions, disciplinary societies, and other organizations that constitute the infrastructure of graduate education to embrace them. As PFF becomes both more widespread and more visible, it will become an ever more potent force in the doctoral preparation of the professoriate.

Although the national PFF program has provided grants to departments and universities to develop PFF programs, several institutions have established PFF programs utilizing only their own resources. For example, Claremont Graduate University, University of Michigan, University of Missouri, Vanderbilt University, and Virginia Commonwealth University all have created their own university-wide programs in the last three years. Typically, leaders at these institutions have had extensive conversations with PFF leaders, often inviting speakers and consultants from other institutions and borrowing from the extensive programmatic resources that have been accumulated. More initiatives of this kind are needed.

Linking PFF to important reforms in undergraduate education

Forces for changing undergraduate education are in motion in both research universities that anchor the clusters and at the partner institutions. These include reforms that promote higher quality and more coherent general education programs. Faculty in science and mathematics are being called on to assist with the development of important skills, such as writing and speaking, analyzing values, and using the computer as a tool for learning. Interdisciplinary learning communities are found in many institutions to personalize education, integrate knowledge across the disciplines, and study problems and issues that transcend individual disciplines. Undergraduate curricula increasingly include courses on aspects of both domestic and global diversity. New faculty need to be active participants in these initiatives.

Improving the quality of undergraduate education is not as simple as establishing learning goals and setting requirements. At a time when nearly 70 percent of high school graduates go on to some form of postsecondary education, professors must address a significant variety of students in terms of preparation, culture, expectations, and aspirations. Professors must be creative, clever, and persistent in both offering intellectual challenges and providing support to their students to meet those challenges.

Regional accrediting bodies are now requiring that colleges and universities assess student learning and demonstrate educational effectiveness as a condition of accreditation. To maintain accreditation, institutions must establish clear learning goals, design curricula to help students achieve those goals, and demonstrate that goals are met. Being responsive to these challenges will require substantial effort and commitment from faculty to a new way of thinking about education. PFF programs can provide the linkage between graduate education and these new challenges for undergraduate education.

Fostering professional development as a component in programs of financial support of graduate students.

Graduate students typically are supported financially by research assistantships, teaching assistantships, and graduate fellowships. Conditions for funding can substantially influence policies and practices at universities. Agencies that support graduate students can therefore promote professional development programs for students by considering such programs as positive factors in funding decisions.

Research assistantships traditionally support learning the protocols and disciplinary practices of conducting research. More professional development opportunities would broaden graduate students' range of competencies and result in more mature researchers. For example, graduate students could be provided opportunities to explore the ethical issues and social implications of their research, provided with information about identifying appropriate programs at funding agencies, and trained in grant writing. They could also be assisted in making presentations of their findings to the public and given guidance about explaining complex phenomena in terms that laypersons understand.

Although excellent teaching assistant development programs do exist, they do not reach all graduate students who could benefit from them, and often they focus on classroom management rather than the intellectual challenges of teaching a range of students.

Teaching assistantships, too often, are seen largely as a way to cover instructional obligations rather than opportunities for graduate students to grow as teachers and scholars (Nyquist, et al. 2001). Although excellent teaching assistant development programs do exist (Marincovich, et al. 1998), they do not reach all graduate students who could benefit from them, and often they focus on classroom management rather than the intellectual challenges of teaching a range of students. If graduate students were introduced to the rich literature on teaching and learning, involved in instructional problems and devising solutions to them, asked to engage their disciplines in regard to relevant social needs and problems, or invited to devise more effective ways of assessing learning than classroom tests, those experiences would provide them with more opportunities to grow as teachers.

Fellowships are highly valued funding mechanisms because they free students from the responsibility to work either in research or teaching. But fellowship holders with an interest in teaching have asked to be included in several PFF programs. They recognize the importance of workshops, seminars, and internships in being prepared and competitive for faculty positions. Inclusion in PFF programs may also help integrate fellowship holders into the social fabric of their graduate programs, as Barbara Lovitts (2001) suggests.

When Syracuse University created its Future Professoriate Project (FPP), it gave participants an opportunity to teach, provided a "teaching mentor," encouraged students to develop a "teaching portfolio," and awarded a Certificate in College Teaching. When the university's fellowship holders found out about this, they wanted to have the same opportunities, so the university developed a modified FPP program for them. Similarly, Howard University requires PFF participation for students funded by all educational grants secured by the Graduate School of Arts and Sciences, because it wants to support the professional development of all its students. These examples illustrate the value of organizations that award graduate fellowships encouraging recipients to take advantage of professional development opportunities. Coincidentally, this would make it necessary for the department to *have* a program for their students.

The postdoctoral experience is becoming more common as preparation for a faculty career, especially in the biological and life sciences. Although many postdoctoral fellows anticipate a career in the academy, their experiences do little to prepare them for any except a research position. Most have few credentials that would qualify them for any faculty job where good teaching is a high priority and where new faculty members are expected to contribute to curricular or institutional initiatives. That is why several post-doctoral fellows—at Duke University and the University of Cincinnati, for example—have been attracted to the PFF programs as core participants. This broader preparation of fellows complements the recent call from the National Academies (Committee on Science, Engineering, and Public Policy 2000) to enhance the postdoctoral experience for scientists and engineers.

We urge graduate faculty members in the sciences and mathematics to consider these ideas and incorporate them into their departmental require-ments for the Ph.D. degree.

A Confluence of Forces for Change

A confluence of forces—including disciplinary societies and departmental clusters involved in this project—has come together in recent years to pro-mote improvement in the preparation of future faculty. All of these efforts are compatible with the vision of PFF, and many are to some extent stimu-lated by PFF. They reinforce each other and collectively point toward a change in the "culture of preparation," not only of future science and mathe-matics faculty, but of all faculty.

▲ Many research studies of graduate students, new faculty, and Ph.D. alumni that empirically document the need for programs like PFF have been completed. For example, the survey of over 32,000 gradu-ate students conducted by the National Association of Graduate and Professional Students (2001) found that fewer than half of respon-dents across all disciplines agreed that teaching assistants are appro-priately prepared and trained before they enter the classroom. Only 52 percent agreed that doctoral students in their programs receive training in ethics and professional responsibilities.

▲ *The Compact for Faculty Diversity* brought together three regional higher educational compacts, Southern Regional Education Board, Western Interstate Commission for Higher Education, and New England Board of Higher Education, for the purpose of preparing more people of color for faculty positions. Working in partnership with the states in their regions, the compacts arranged for financial support of doctoral education for hundreds of individuals and provided them with faculty mentors and professional development experiences.

▲ *The Re-envisioning the Ph.D.* project allowed Jody Nyquist and a small staff at the University of Washington to collect a wealth of information about graduate education—data about its strengths and weaknesses, criticisms and calls for change, innovations, initiatives of disciplinary associations, needs of colleges and universities as well as businesses that hire Ph.D.s, fellowship programs, and others. A major national conference brought together all major constituencies to discuss specific actions that each group could take to improve graduate preparation—graduate students, graduate faculty, colleges and universities that hire new faculty, disciplinary societies, fellowship providers, educational associations, businesses, and government agencies. The rich repository of resources from these activities is available on the Web site www.grad.washington.edu/envision/.

▲ *The Forum on Faculty Roles and Rewards* of the American Association for Higher Education has become a clearinghouse of information about the changing roles of faculty. Eugene Rice and his colleagues have made it the premier intellectual center for broadening the definition of scholarship, studying transitions in faculty roles throughout the academic career, and analyzing such aspects of faculty working conditions as post-tenure review, faculty reward systems, and tenure—all of which inform doctoral preparation.

▲ *Preparing Future Professionals* programs have been launched at many universities to prepare graduate students for positions outside the academy. The logic is that if it is good to acquaint graduate students seeking a faculty position with a variety of colleges and universities, then it also would be helpful to give those students seeking non-academic careers a chance to explore opportunities in organizations where they might work. Programs such as these have been developed at universities where PFF programs flourish, such as Arizona State University, University of Minnesota, and University of Texas, Austin.

▲ *The Responsive PhD* is a project of the Woodrow Wilson National Fellowship Foundation. Under the leadership of President Robert Weisbuch, it has selected a group of fourteen doctoral universities (nine of them involved in the PFF program) to hold a series of forums to devise ways to create a doctorate that is more responsive to social and academic changes. In particular, it is addressing new paradigms (including interdisciplinarity and scholarship that emphasize national and community issues), new practices (including preparation for teaching and other forms of professional development), and new people (including service to more diverse populations and diversifying the American intellect).

▲ *Pedagogies of the Disciplines* is an initiative of the Carnegie Foundation for the Advancement of Teaching. It emphasizes "stewardship of the discipline" in six different fields. Led by George

Walker, a prominent leader of PFF at Indiana University, it will commission essays on central aspects of the disciplines, encourage groups of faculty members to consider improvements in doctoral education, support innovations, and study the consequences of the new practices. It seeks nothing less than to embed the scholarship of teaching and learning, championed by Carnegie president Lee Shulman and his colleagues, into the heart of doctoral education.

These several initiatives, based on a growing body of research, hold promise for developing more welcoming, more informative, and more supportive pathways for graduate students to become faculty members. These important initiatives and other variations on PFF themes will contribute to a broader vision of graduate education, incorporating many of the values of PFF. Because the disciplinary societies and clusters in this project have gained experience with PFF, have come to see its benefits, and have vowed to stay the course, we are optimistic about the future of Preparing Future Faculty.

Several initiatives ... hold promise for developing more welcoming, more informative, and more supportive pathways for graduate students to become faculty members.

If this optimism is warranted, if PFF programs become a new standard for faculty preparation, then four consequences may be expected to follow. First, a transformation will take place in the culture of doctoral preparation from one based solely on research preparation to one that includes preparation for a range of professional responsibilities. Graduate students seeking an academic career will begin to learn about teaching and professional service as well as research and to balance and integrate these several responsibilities.

Second, PFF will foster a closer collaboration between doctoral degree-granting universities and the institutions that hire new doctoral degree holders and mostly emphasize undergraduate education. This will bring the realities of undergraduate education—its rationale, challenges, successes, and alternatives—into dialogue with graduate education that is reshaping itself to better prepare faculty.

Third, new faculty will have a better understanding of the academic profession and of the institutions where it is practiced. If new faculty members understand how institutions of higher learning work, they will be better able to use organizations to create conditions of learning for their students and better working conditions for themselves and their colleagues.

Finally, all of this adds up to better education for students, whether undergraduate or graduate. Faculty in the future will be able to create learning communities that are effective for future generations of students, and the as-yet-unknown futures that they will face.

Appendix I

Graduate Students and Postdoctorates from Phase 3 PFF Disciplines

This appendix places the Phase 3 PFF project in the sciences and mathematics within the larger context of graduate education. In 1998, graduate enrollment in science disciplines (NSF 2002a) was approximately 17 percent of total (NCES 2002). However, about half of all Ph.D. degrees conferred between July 1, 1999 and June 30, 2000 (FY2000) were in the sciences (NSF 2001).

Table I provides data on graduate enrollment and postdoctorates in fall 2000 (NSF 2002a) and Ph.D. degrees awarded in FY 2000 (NSF 2001) for all science disciplines and for each of the PFF phase 3 disciplines. Table I reveals that the PFF phase 3 disciplines enroll almost half of all science graduate students and award nearly two-thirds of science Ph.D. degrees. Biological sciences enroll more than 56,000 graduate students, computer science over 47,000, and the other fields combined over 45,000. Biological sciences support more postdoctorates and award more Ph.D. degrees than the other PFF phase 3 disciplines combined. According to Robert Beck, a member of the Special Interest Group on Computer Science Education (SIGCSE) of the Association of Computing Machinery (ACM), the small number of Ph.D. degrees awarded in computer science, compared to the sizable graduate enrollment, reflects the robust employment market for computer science master's graduates.

Table 1. Graduate Enrollment, Ph.D. degrees awarded, and Postdoctoral Appointments, by discipline[1]

Discipline	Graduate Enrollment	Ph.D. Degrees	Postdoctoral Appointments
All Fields	1,767,557[2]	41,368	N/A
All Sciences	309,969	20,649	25,745
Biological Sciences	56,494	5,855	16,093
Mathematical Sciences	15,646	1,048	375
Computer Sciences	47,594	861	352
Chemistry	18,188	1,990	3,574
Physics/Astronomy	11,724	1,392	2,176
Totals, PFF3 Disciplines	**149,646**	**13,055**	**22,570**
Among All Sciences	48.3%	63.2%	87.7%
Among All Fields	9.9%	31.6%	N/A

[1]Except where otherwise noted, data are from NSF 2002a (graduate enrollment and postdoctoral appointments, Fall 2000) and NSF 2001 (Ph.D. degrees, 1999-2000)
[2]NCES 2002 (total graduate enrollment, all fields, Fall 1998)

The *Biological Sciences* encompass a broad range of distinct disciplines, from entomology to neuroscience, from structural biology to ecology. Doctoral programs may be located in colleges of arts and science, agriculture, or medicine/health. The career paths for biological science graduates vary by specialization: For example, biochemistry Ph.D. graduates may have more opportunities for non-academic positions than those from ecology, because of the large numbers of career opportunities in biotechnology and pharmaceutical industries.

The National Research Council has studied the career paths of biological sciences graduates since the 1970s (NRC 1998). They found that, on average, approximately 60 percent of doctoral graduates in the biological sciences have pursued postdoctoral appointments and that many employers expect this experience. Further, about 40 percent of biological science Ph.D.s in the NRC study ultimately obtained tenure-track academic positions; of these, more than 85 percent were in Ph.D. granting institutions, many in basic science departments in medical schools.

Although many biological science graduate students have opportunities to serve as teaching assistants, those in departments located in a college of medicine or agriculture often are supported solely by research grants and hence have no opportunity to teach or learn about the professoriate, except through PFF programs.

Almost three-quarters of *Chemistry* Ph.D. graduates (1,990 in 2000) take jobs—including postdoctoral positions—in business and industry, according to Jerry Bell of the American Chemical Society. Those who obtain academic positions are broadly distributed among the diverse institutions of higher education. Many chemistry graduate students serve as teaching assistants, often in laboratory courses. Few have the opportunity to gain experience in classroom teaching. Thus, PFF is an important complement to the normal graduate experience of chemistry graduate students.

A total of 861 *Computer Science* degrees were awarded in 2000, about 35 percent to international students. Because of the explosive growth of the discipline and the strong demand from business, most computer science graduates enter the workforce after either an undergraduate or a master's degree. According to Robert Beck (SIGCSE/ACM), among Ph.D. graduates, only about one-third obtain an academic position; as a result, approximately

700 faculty openings annually either remain unfilled or are filled by computer science master's graduates or by master's or Ph.D. graduates from related fields.

Of the 1,048 Ph.D. degrees awarded in *Mathematics* in 2000, about half were earned by international students, 22 percent of whom indicated immediate plans to seek employment outside the U.S. (presumably, many of these planned to return to their home country), and 24 percent had immediate plans to join the U.S. work force—12 percent each in academic positions and in industry (NSF 2001). Among the 1999-2000 Ph.D. mathematics graduates with definite plans for U.S. employment following graduation (63 percent overall; 45 percent of international graduates), 40 percent had academic positions (25 percent of international graduates); 33 percent had post-doctoral positions (45 percent of international graduates); and roughly 20 percent planned to enter industry (26 percent of international graduates). The remainder reported other U.S. employment (NSF 2001).

According to Samuel M. Rankin, III, of the American Mathematical Society, most mathematicians seek employment immediately after the Ph.D., and taking a post-doctoral appointment is a much less common option. Eventually, about 75 percent of doctoral graduates who reside in the United States obtain faculty positions, primarily in four-year colleges.

Most mathematics graduate students serve as teaching assistants for some portion or most of their graduate program. Experienced teaching assistants commonly are given sole responsibility for an entire course. Consequently, many mathematics departments have a teaching assistant training program, and faculty and students tend to be particularly supportive of PFF programs.

Physics and Astronomy awarded 1,392 Ph.D. degrees in 2000, about half to international students, only 10 percent of whom indicated immediate plans to seek employment outside the U.S.; presumably, for many of these, in their home country. Among 1999-2000 Ph.D. physics graduates with definite immediate post-graduation plans for U.S. employment (56 percent of the total), 48 percent had obtained academic positions (3 percent of international graduates); about 60 percent of both U.S. and of international graduates planned to take postdoctoral positions and postpone entry into the workforce; and approximately 33 percent of both groups planned to take employment in industry (NSF 2001).

As a result of a declining production of Ph.D. physicists and increasing retirements among Sputnik-generation faculty, the current academic job market is more favorable than at any time in the last ten years, reports Warren Hein of the American Association of Physics Teachers, making PFF programs in physics especially valuable and timely.

Appendix II

PFF3 Faculty Leaders and Partner Institutions

Biological and Life Sciences

Duke University

Paula Lemons, Assistant Professor of the Practice, Duke University, Department of Biology, Box 90338, Durham, NC 27708-0338, Ph: (919) 668-6181, Fax: (919) 660-7293, E-mail: plemons@duke.edu

Partner Institutions: North Carolina Central University, Guilford College, Durham Technical Community College, Elon University, Meredith College

University of Cincinnati

Carl A. Huether, Professor, University of Cincinnati, Department of Biological Sciences, P.O. Box 210006, Cincinnati, OH 45221-0006, Ph: (513) 556-9764, Fax: (513) 556-5299, E-mail: carl.heuther@uc.edu

Partner Institutions: Raymond Walters College, College of Mount Saint Joseph, Northern Kentucky University, Xavier University

University of Nebraska, Lincoln

Leon Higley, Professor, University of Nebraska, Department of Entomology, 303A Plant Industry Building, Lincoln, NE 68583-0816, Ph: (402)

472-8689, Fax: (402) 472-4687, E-mail: lhigley1@unl.edu

Partner Institutions: Alcorn State University, Concordia College, Creighton University, Dana College, Doane College, Grambling State University, Metropolitan Community College, Nebraska Wesleyan University, New Mexico Highlands University, University of Nebraska at Omaha

University of South Carolina

Tom Reeves, Professor, Midlands Technical College, Department of Biology, Airport Campus, Robinson Building—Room 108, Columbia, SC 29202, Ph: (803) 822-3554, Fax: (803) 822-3422, E-mail: reevest@mid-landstech.com

Partner Institutions: Benedict College, Midlands Technical College, South Carolina Commission on Higher Education, University of South Carolina-Salkehatchie

Chemistry

Duquesne University

David W. Seybert, Professor, Duquesne University, Department of Chemistry and Biochemistry, 308 Mellon Hall, Pittsburgh, PA 15282, Ph: (412) 396-6465, Fax: (412) 396-5683, E-mail: seybert@duq.edu

Partner Institutions: Chatham College, Seton Hill College, St. Vincent's College, Thiel College, West Liberty State College

Queens College of the City University of New York

Thomas C. Strekas, Acting Dean, Queens College of the City University of New York, Division of Mathematics and Natural Sciences, 65-30 Kissena Boulevard, Flushing, NY 11367-1547, Ph: (718) 997-4105,

Fax: (718) 997-4103, E-mail: thomas_strekas@qc.edu or
tcsqc@forbin.qc.edu

Partner Institutions: Baruch College, Manhattan College, Queensborough
Community College

University of California-Los Angeles

Arlene A. Russell, Senior Lecturer, University of California-Los Angeles,
Department of Chemistry and Biochemistry, 607 Charles E. Young
Drive East, Box 951569, Los Angeles, CA 90095-1569, Ph: (310) 825-
7570, Fax: (310) 825-4795, E-mail: russell@chem.ucla.edu

Partner Institutions: California State University-Fullerton, Mount San
Antonio College, Mount St. Mary's College, Pierce College, Pomona
College

University of Massachusetts-Amherst

Julian F. Tyson, Professor, University of Massachusetts at Amherst,
Department of Chemistry, 701 Lederle Graduate Research Tower, 710
North Pleasant St., Amherst, MA 01003-9336, Ph: (413) 545-0195,
Fax: (413) 545-4846, E-mail: tyson@chem.umass.edu

Partner Institutions: Amherst College, Hampshire College, Greenfield
Community College, Mt. Holyoke College, Smith College, Holyoke
Community College

University of Michigan

Brian P. Coppola, Associate Professor, University of Michigan, Department
of Chemistry, 930 North University Avenue, 2403 Chemistry Building,
Ann Arbor, MI 48109-1055, Ph: (734) 764-7329, Fax: (734) 647-4865,

E-mail: bcoppola@umich.edu

Partner Institutions: Baldwin-Wallace College, Calvin College, Eastern Michigan University, Grand Valley State University, Hillsdale College, Hope College, Oakland University, Oberlin College

Computer Science
University of Cincinnati

Carla Purdy, Associate Professor, University of Cincinnati, Electronic Design Automation Research Center, ECECS Department, ML 30, Cincinnati, OH 45221-0030, Ph: (513) 556-1810, Fax: (513) 556-7326, E-mail: Carla.Purdy@uc.edu

Partner Institutions: College of Mount Saint Joseph, Northern Kentucky University, Xavier University

University of Iowa

Steve Bruell, University of Iowa, Department of Computer Science, 14 MacLean Hall, Iowa City, IA 52242-1419, Ph: (319) 335-0713, Fax: (319) 335-3624, E-mail: bruell@cs.uiowa.edu

Partner Institutions: Central College, Cornell College, Grinnell College, St. Ambrose University

Mathematics
Arizona State University

Dieter Armbruster, Professor, Arizona State University, Department of Mathematics, College of Liberal Arts and Sciences, Tempe, AZ 85287-1804, Ph: (480) 965-5441, Fax: (480) 965-8119, E-mail: dieter@math.la.asu.edu

Partner Institutions: Arizona State University-West, Northern Arizona
University, Scottsdale Community College

Binghamton University

Luise-Charlotte Kappe, Binghamton University, Mathematics Department,
Vestal Parkway East, P.O. Box 6000, Binghamton, NY 13902, Ph:
(607) 777-2355, Fax: (607) 777-2450, E-mail: menger@math.bing-
hamton.edu

Partner Institutions: Broome Community College, Ithaca College, King's
College, SUNY-Oneonta

University of Washington

Virginia M. Warfield, Senior Lecturer, University of Washington,
Department of Mathematics, Mail Stop 354350, Seattle, WA 98195,
Ph: (206) 543-7445, Fax: (206) 543-0397, E-mail:
warfield@math.washington.edu

Partner Institutions: Seattle University, Seattle Central Community College

Virginia Polytechnic Institute and State University

Robert C. Rogers, Graduate Program Director, Virginia Polytechnic Institute
and State University, Department of Mathematics, 530 McBryde Hall,
Blacksburg, VA 24061-0123, Ph:(540) 231-4184, Fax:(540) 231-5960,
E-mail: rogers@vt.edu

Partner Institutions: Bridgewater College, High Point University, Virginia
State University, Washington and Lee University

Physics

Howard University

Yehuda Salu, Professor, Howard University, Department of Physics and
Astronomy, 201 Thirkield Hall, 2355 6th Street NW, Washington, DC
20059, Ph: (202) 806-6025, Fax: (202) 806-5830, E-mail:
ysalu@howard.edu

Partner Institutions: Bowie State University, The Catholic University of
America, Howard Community College, Marymount University,
Virginia Tech-Northern Virginia Campus

University of Arkansas

Gay B. Stewart, Associate Professor of Physics, University of Arkansas,
Fayetteville, Department of Physics, 226 Physics Building, Fayetteville,
AR 72701, Ph: (479) 575-2408, Fax: (479) 575-4580, E-mail: gstew-
art@uark.edu

Partner Institutions: Crowder College, Drury University, Northwest
Arkansas Community College, University of Arkansas-Ft. Smith,
University of Kansas

University of California, San Diego

Rosalind Streichler, Director, Center for Teaching Development, University
of California, San Diego, 307 Center Hall – Mail Code 0030, La Jolla,
CA 92093-0030, Ph: (858) 534-3958, Fax: (858) 822-0318, E-mail:
rstreichler@ucsd.edu

Partner Institutions: Grossmont College, San Diego City College, San Diego
State University, University of San Diego

University of Colorado at Boulder

John Cumalat, Professor, University of Colorado at Boulder, Department of
  Physics, Campus Box 390, Boulder, CO 80309-0390, Ph: (303) 492-
  8604, Fax: (303) 492-3352, E-mail: jcumalat@pizero.colorado.edu

Partner Institutions: Adams State College, Colorado College, Colorado
  School of Mines, Colorado State University, Denver University,
  Metropolitan State College of Denver, United States Air Force Academy,
  University of Wyoming

References

Adams, K.A. 2002. *What colleges and universities want in new faculty.* Preparing Future Faculty Occasional Paper Number 7. Washington, DC: Association of American Colleges and Universities and Council of Graduate Schools.

American Association of Physics Teachers. n.d. *Preparing future physics faculty.* College Park, MD: American Association of Physics Teachers.

American Council on Education. 2001. *Higher Education and National Affairs.* October 22, 3.

Applegate, J.L. 2002. *Engaged graduate education: Seeing with new eyes.* Preparing Future Faculty Occasional Paper Number 9. Washington, DC: Association of American Colleges and Universities and Council of Graduate Schools.

Astin, A.A. 1993. *What matters in college.* San Francisco: Jossey-Bass.

Austin, A.E. 2002. Preparing the next generation of faculty: Graduate school as socialization to the academic career. *Journal of Higher Education*, 73: 1, 94-122.

Bogle, E. 2001. Experiences at Catholic University. *Beyond Research* 5. http://www.founders.howard.edu/gsas/pff/pff_newsletter.htm

Bransford, J.D., A.L. Brown, and R.R. Cocking, eds. 1999. How people learn: Brain, mind, experience, and school. Washington, DC: National Academy Press.

CGS/GRE Survey of Graduate Enrollment. 1998. Washington, DC: Council of Graduate Schools.

Chickering, A.W. and Z. Gamson. 1987. Seven principles for good practice in undergraduate education. *AAHE Bulletin*. Washington, DC: American Association for Higher Education.

Chism, N.Van N. and A.S. Pruitt. 1995. Promoting inclusiveness in college teaching. In W.A. Wright, ed. *Teaching improvement practices: successful strategies for higher education*. Bolton, MA: Anker, 325-345.

Cody, J.A. 2001. From PFF fellow to faculty mentor. Presentation at Preparing Future Faculty Symposium at American Chemical Society. Chicago.

Committee on Graduate Education. 1998. *Report and recommendations*. Washington, DC: Association of American Universities.

Committee on Science, Engineering and Public Policy (COSEPUP). 1995. *Reshaping the education of scientists and engineers*. Washington, DC: National Academy Press.

Committee on Science, Engineering, and Public Policy (COSEPUP). 2000. *Enhancing the postdoctoral experience for scientists and engineers*. Washington, DC: National Academy Press.

Commonwealth Partnership. 1996. *What you should know: An open letter to new Ph.D.s.* Lancaster, PA: Franklin and Marshall College.

DeNeef, A.L. 2002. *The Preparing Future Faculty program: What difference does it make?* Preparing Future Faculty Occasional Paper Number 8. Washington, DC: Association of American Colleges and Universities and Council of Graduate Schools.

Gaff, J.G. and J.L.Ratcliff. 1997. *Handbook of the undergraduate curriculum*. San Francisco: Jossey-Bass.

Golde, C.M. and T. M. Dore. 2001. *At cross purposes: What the experiences of today's graduate students reveal about doctoral education.* Philadelphia: The Pew Charitable Trusts.

Hoffer, T., B. Dugoni, A. Sanderson, S. Sederstrom, R. Ghadialy, P. Pocque. 2001. *Doctorate recipients from United States Universities: Summary Report 2000.* Chicago: National Opinion Research Center. (Produced by NORC for NSF, NIH,USED,NEH, USDA, AND NASA.) www.nsf.gov/sbe/srs/sendgr/start.htm

Hunt, S.W. and A.T. Schwartz. 2001. Preparing Future Faculty: Musings of a mentee and mentor. Presentation at Preparing Future Faculty Symposium. Chicago.

López, C. 1999. A decade of assessing student learning: What we have learned. What's Next? Presented at the 104th Annual Meeting of the North Central Association/Commission on Institutions of Higher Education. Available on line: www.ncahigherlearningcommission.org/resources/assessment/index.html

Lovitts, B.E. 2001. *Leaving the ivory tower.* New York: Rowman & Littlefield.

Marincovich, M., J. Prostco, and F. Stout, eds. 1998. *The professional development of graduate teaching assistants.* Bolton, MA: Anker Publishing Co.

McKeachie, W.J. 1999. *Teaching tips* (10th edition). Boston: Houghton Mifflin Company.

Menges, R.J., M. Weimer, and Associates. 1996. *Teaching on solid ground: Using scholarship to improve practice.* San Francisco: Jossey-Bass.

National Association of Graduate and Professional Students. 2001. Preliminary executive summary of the National Doctoral Program Survey. Washington, DC. http://survey.nagaps.org

National Research Council. 1998. *Trends in the early careers of life scientists*, Appendix F. Washington, DC: National Academy Press.

National Science Foundation. Division of Science Resource Statistics. 2002a. *Graduate students and postdoctorates in science and engineering: Fall 2000*. NSF 02-314. Arlington, VA: National Science Foundation. www.bsf.gov/sbe/srs/stats.htm

National Science Foundation. 2002b. Academic employment of doctoral scientists and engineers, by degree field, race/ethnicity, and type of position: 1973-99. *Science and engineering indicators 2002*, Volume 2, Appendix table (5-31). Arlington, VA: National Science Foundation. www.nsf.gov/sbe/srs/seind02/pdf_v2.htm

National Science Foundation. 2002c. Retention in science and engineering. *Science and engineering indicators 2002.* Volume 2. Arlington, VA: National Science Foundation. www.nsf.gov/sbe/srs/seind02/c2/c2st.htm

National Science Foundation. Division of Science Resource Statistics. 2001. *Science and engineering doctorate awards: 2000.* NSF 02-305. Arlington, VA: National Science Foundation. www.nsf.gov/sbe/srs/stats.htm

National Science Foundation. 2000. *Land of plenty: Diversity in America's competitive edge in science, engineering and technology.* Arlington, VA: National Science Foundation.

National Science Foundation Advisory Committee to the Directorate for Education and Human Resources. 1996. *Shaping the future: New expectations for undergraduate education in science, mathematics, engineering, and technology.* Arlington, VA: National Science Foundation.

Nerad, M. and J. Cerney. 2000. Improving doctoral education: Recommendations from the Ph.D.'s—Ten Years Later Study. *Communicator* 33: 2, 6.

Nerad, M., and J. Cerney. 1999. From rumors to facts: Career outcomes of English Ph.D.s. *Communicator* 32:7.

Nyquist, J.D., A.E. Austin, J. Sprague, and D.H. Wulff. 2001. *The development of graduate students as teaching scholars: A four-year longitudinal study.* Center for Instructional Development and Research. Seattle, WA: University of Washington.

Pascarella, E.T.and P.T.Terenzini. 1991. *How college affects students.* San Francisco: Jossey-Bass.

Pruitt-Logan, A.S., J.G.Gaff, and R.A.Weibl. 1998. *The impact: Assessing experiences of participants in the Preparing Future Faculty program, 1994-1996.* Preparing Future Faculty Occasional Paper Number 6. Washington, DC: Association of American Colleges and Universities.

Rice, R.E., M.D. Sorcinelli, and A.E.Austin. 2000. *Heeding new voices: Academic careers for a new generation.* New Pathways Working Papers Series #7. Washington, DC: American Association for Higher Education.

Seymour, E. 2002. Tracking the processes of change in U.S. undergraduate education in science, mathematics, engineering, and technology. *Science Education,* 86:1, 79- 105.

Smith, S.J. and L. Pedersen-Gallegos. 2001. The careers and work of Ph.D. scientists: Not simply academic. Unpublished paper. Boulder: University of Colorado Bureau of Sociological Research, Department of Sociology.

Sorcinelli, M.D. 2001. Paradise lost: How the academy converts enthusiastic recruits into early-career doubters. Presentation at AAHE Conference on Faculty Roles and Rewards. Tampa, Florida.

Survey of Earned Doctorates 2000. 2001. Conducted under the direction of the National Science Foundation, National Institutes of Health, U.S. Department of Education, National Endowment for the Humanities, U.S. Department of Agriculture, and the National Aeronautics and Space Administration. Chicago: National Opinion Research Center.

Thomas, V.G. 2002. *Evaluation report of shaping the preparation of science and mathematics faculty project.* Washington, DC: Council of Graduate Schools and Association of American Colleges and Universities,

Trower, C.A. 2001. Paradise lost: How the academy converts enthusiastic recruits into early-career doubters. Presentation at AAHE Conference on Faculty Roles and Rewards. Tampa, Florida.

U.S. Department of Education, National Center for Education Statistics, [E.D.Tabs]. *Fall enrollment in Title IV degree-granting postsecondary institutions: 1998*, NCES, 2002-162, Table IV, by Frank B. Morgan. Washington, DC: National Center for Education Statistics.

Wubbels, G.G., and J.S.Girgus. 1997. The natural sciences and mathematics. In J.G. Gaff and J.L. Ratcliff, eds. *Handbook of the undergraduate curriculum.* San Francisco: Jossey-Bass, 280-300.

Web Resources

American Association of Physics Teachers (AAPT): www.aapt.org/

American Chemical Society (ACS): www.acs.org

Association of Computing Machinery/Special Interest Group on Computer
Science Education (ACM/SIGCSE): www.acm.org/sigcas/

American Mathematical Society (AMS): http://e-math.ams.org/

Binghamton University. Survey of PFF participants: www.math.bingham-
ton.edu/pff/

Department of Education Graduate Assistance in Areas of National Need
(GAANN): www.ed.gov/offices/OPE/HEP/iegps/gaann.html

Mathematical Association of America (MAA): www.maa.org/

NSF Alliances for Graduate Education and the Professoriate (AGEP):
www.her.nsf.gov/her/hrd/agep.asp

National Science Foundation (NSF) Integrative Graduate Education and
Research Training (IGERT): www.nsf.gov/igert

National Science Foundation (NSF) Louis Stokes Alliances for Minority
Participation Program (LSAMP): www.ehr.nsf.gov/hrd/amp.asp

Preparing Future Faculty: www.preparing-faculty.org

University of California at San Diego, Center for Teaching Development.
Detailed criteria for gaining the CTD Certificate in College and
University Teaching: http://ctd.ucsd.edu/PFPF/activityCourse.html

University of California at San Diego. Preparing Future Physics Faculty:
www-ctd.ucsd.edu/PFPF/index.html

University of Cincinnati. Preparing Future Faculty in the Life Sciences:
www.uc.edu/pffls

The Council of Graduate Schools (CGS) is dedicated to the improvement and advancement of graduate education. Its members are colleges and universities engaged in research, scholarship and the preparation of candidates for advanced degrees. As the largest national association organized specifically to represent the interests of graduate education, CGS offers many opportunities for deans and graduate school personnel to exchange ideas and share information on major issues in graduate education. Over 400 U.S., Canadian and international institutions are represented in the CGS membership. www.cgsnet.org

Association of American Colleges and Universities

AAC&U is the leading national association devoted to advancing and strengthening liberal learning for all students, regardless of academic specialization or intended career. Since its founding in 1915, AAC&U's membership has grown to nearly 800 accredited public and private colleges and universities of every type and size.

AAC&U functions as a catalyst and facilitator, forging links among presidents, administrators, and faculty members who are engaged in institutional and curricular planning. Its mission is to reinforce the collective commitment to liberal education at both the national and local levels and to help individual institutions keep the quality of student learning at the core of their work as they evolve to meet new economic and social challenges. www.aacu.org